PASS THE U.S. CITIZENSHIP EXAM

Mary Masi

with the assistance of

MINNESOTA LITERACY COUNCIL
St. Paul, Minnesota

CATHOLIC CHARITIES IMMIGRATION AND REFUGEE SERVICES
Harrisburg, Pennsylvania

McDONAUGH ORGANIZATION WITH RESPECT AND
EQUALITY FOR PEOPLE (MORE)
St. Paul, Minnesota

LEARNINGEXPRESS

New York

Library of Congress Cataloging-in-Publication Data
Masi, Mary.
    Pass the U.S. citizenship exam / by Mary Masi.
      p.   cm.
    ISBN 1–57685–222–9
    1. Citizenship—United States—Examinations Study guides.   I. Title.
JK1758.M37   1999
326.23'0973—dc21

99-20290
CIP

Printed in the United States of America
9 8 7 6 5 4 3 2 1
First Edition

Portions of this guide have been adapted from *Citizenship*, provided by the Minnesota Literacy Council © 1997. Additional material was adapted from *Study Guide to Prepare for New Written Citizenship Examination: A Guide for Beginner Level ESL Students*, provided by Catholic Charities Immigration and Refugee Services of Harrisburg, PA.

Regarding the Information in this Book

We attempt to verify the information presented in our books prior to publication. It is always a good idea, however, to double-check application and testing procedures with the Immigration and Naturalization Service, as such information can change from time to time. This book does not provide legal advice. For help with your immigration status, consult a lawyer.

For Further Information

For information on LearningExpress, other LearningExpress products, or bulk sales, please write to us at:
    LearningExpress®
    900 Broadway
    Suite 604
    New York, NY 10003

ISBN 1–57685–222–9

7 85555 85222 8

Table of Contents

CONTRIBUTORS

LearningExpress thanks the following individuals and organizations for their contributions to the content of this book.

Laura Jaeger, Executive Director, and **LeeAnn Wolf,** Citizenship Coordinator, of the Minnesota Literacy Council (MLC).

Norman Lederer, Director; **Judy Sides,** ESL Program Director; **Annabelle Saylor,** author; and **Douglas Nannen,** author, from the Diocese of Harrisburg, Pennsylvania, Catholic Charities Immigration and Refugee Services (CCIRS).

Sr. Audrey Lindenfelser, SSND, Coordinator Citizenship from the McDonaugh Organization with Respect and Equality for People (MORE) of St. Paul, Minnesota.

Mary Masi, M.A., author and editor from Clearwater, Florida.

Karen Williams-Jones, Spanish instructor and Ph.D. candidate at Yale University.

NOTE TO TEACHERS AND TUTORS

Instructor's Guide

An instructor's guide is available from the publisher of this book; you can order a copy by calling LearningExpress at 1-800-295-9556. The *Instructor's Guide: Pass the U.S. Citizenship Exam* (ISBN: 1-57685-229-6) offers instructors teaching tips, ideas for group activities, and background information for each lesson. Instructors will find additional information on civics and historical events to help them clearly explain and "tell the story" of key incidents to their students. Warm-up activities are suggested, and specific learning activities are described. Instructors can choose from a variety of teaching methods and supplemental activities to tailor each lesson to fit the needs of their specific class.

Role of Instructor

Instructors play an important role in helping students achieve the knowledge they need to take and pass the citizenship exam. However, the citizenship or ESL instructor must remember to distinguish between the educational and the legal aspects of citizenship preparation and never give legal advice to students. When you are approached by students with legal questions regarding their immigrant status, be prepared with the names and phone numbers of local legal-aid agencies, phone hotlines, or experienced immigration attorneys.

Dated Material

While your students may have varying levels of United States history and civics education, in this book they will find all the material they need to pass the citizenship exam. However, as you begin teaching the material in this book, keep in mind that some information may go out of date, such as the intricacies of applying for naturalization or the name of the U.S. President.

How to Use This Book

This book can help you pass the United States Citizenship Exam. It also shows you the process of how to become a United States citizen. However, this book does not give legal advice. Go to your lawyer for help with immigration law. You may want to study this book by yourself, with a partner, or in a formal classroom. The book is written for people whose first language is not English.

WHAT YOU WILL FIND IN THIS BOOK

Chapter 1 shows you the good and bad things about getting U.S. citizenship. You should know why you want to become a U.S. citizen. Chapter 2 explains what you need to do to become a U.S. citizen. Remember that naturalization laws can change. Ask your lawyer or someone from the Immigration and Naturalization Service (INS) for updated information. Chapter 3 shows you which INS regional office you should contact for more information or to send your completed N-400 application form.

Chapter 4 is the longest chapter in the book. Chapter 4 has twenty-three lessons in it. Each lesson begins with a list of INS questions that you should learn the answers to. On the next page of the lesson are words that may be new to you. Look at this list of words and read what each word means before beginning the lesson. Also look at the words in the boxes at the beginning of each lesson. Those words show you what that lesson is about.

The lessons give you information you'll need to know to pass the citizenship exam. After you study the information, do the exercise of test questions to make sure you remember the information. Answers to all the exercises in Chapter 4 are in the back of the book (Appendix A). Don't look at the answers until after you try to answer each question.

Each lesson gives dictation practice. Dictation is when the INS person says a sentence out loud and you write it down. You'll also get interview practice in each lesson. First you'll practice reading sample interview questions and answers, and then you'll practice saying your own answers.

There are six review tests that are mixed in with the lessons. Take each review test as you come to it. The answers to the review tests are also in the back of the book.

Chapter 5 is a list of all the words from the twenty-three lessons in Chapter 4 that you may need help with. Next to each word, you'll find the Spanish translation of the word. Then you'll see what the word means in English. All of these words appear in Chapter 4. The words are in alphabetical order (from A–Z).

Chapter 6 is a list of the 100 official INS history and civics questions and answers, arranged by subject. All of these questions and answers are from Chapter 4. Read Chapter 6 whenever you want to review the questions about U.S. history and government. Cover the answers, so you can test yourself. Then look to see if you got the right answer.

Chapter 7 shows you many sample questions and answers from the N-400 "Application for Naturalization" form. These are questions the INS person may ask at your interview. Think about how you would answer each question before you look at the sample answer. All of these sample questions and answers are from Chapter 4.

Chapter 8 gives all the dictation sentences in Chapter 4 in one list. You can practice writing each sentence in the space on the opposite page.

Appendix A, at the back of the book, is a list of all the answers to the exercises and review tests in Chapter 4. Appendix B is a copy of the N-400 "Application for Naturalization" for you to practice filling out.

CHAPTER 1

Do You Want to Be a Citizen?

Many people want to become American citizens. Other people do not. There are many reasons why people want to become American citizens. Think about why you want to become a United States citizen. An American citizen is the same as a United States citizen.

☆ REASONS TO BECOME A CITIZEN

Here are some good things you can get from becoming a United States citizen. Think about what the things below mean to you. Make a check mark next to the things that you want.

_____You get the right to vote in elections.
_____You get to run for public office.
_____You get to apply for jobs with the government.
_____You get to ask for your close family members to come to America legally.
_____Your family members may get to come to America more quickly.
_____More of your family members may get to come to America.
_____Your unmarried children may become citizens.
_____You may get Social Security benefits even if you live in another country.
_____You get to live outside the United States without losing your citizenship.
_____You get to travel with a United States passport.
_____You get to re-enter the United States more easily.
_____You don't have to renew a green card.

_____You don't have to report a change of address.
_____You will not be deported.
_____You get more benefits from the government.
_____You don't have to worry about new immigration laws.

☆ REASONS NOT TO BECOME A CITIZEN

There are a few reasons that you might not want to become a United States citizen. Think about these before you apply to become a citizen. (Some of these things may not apply to you if you can keep dual citizenship. Dual citizenship means you can be a citizen of the United States and a citizen of your native country.) Make a check mark next to the things that you do not want.

_____You must take an Oath of Allegiance to America.
_____You may have to turn your back on your native country.
_____You may have to refuse to help your native country.
_____You may lose your citizenship in your native country.
_____You may lose your property in your native country.
_____You may lose the right to vote in your native country.
_____You must pass a short test about United States government and history.
_____You may be deported if you lie on your application for citizenship.
_____You may be denied citizenship if you lied to get permanent residency in America.

Now look at how many check marks you made. Are there more on the first list? Then you may want to become a U.S. citizen. Are there more check marks on the last list? Then you need to find out if you can get dual citizenship.

For many people, the reasons to become a U.S. citizen are stronger than the reasons not to. Think about why you want to become a U.S. citizen. You may need to answer this question in your INS interview:

Why do you want to become a United States citizen?

CHAPTER 2

The Process of Becoming a Citizen

This chapter will show you how you can become a United States citizen. There are many steps to this process. It may take several months to complete all the steps. Read this chapter carefully.

☆ ARE YOU READY?

Find out if you are ready to apply for U.S. citizenship. If you can answer **Yes** to all of these questions, then you are ready. Circle either **Yes** or **No.**

Yes   No   Are you at least eighteen (18) years old?

Yes   No   Have you been a lawful Permanent Resident of the United States either for five (5) years, OR for three (3) years if you have been married for three years to a person who has been a U.S. citizen for at least three years?

Yes   No   Have you been physically present in the United States for at least 2 1/2 years, OR 1 1/2 years if you are married to a U.S. citizen?

Yes   No   Have you lived within a state or district for at least three (3) months?

Yes   No   Are you willing to swear loyalty to the United States?

Yes   No   Do you have good moral character?

Yes   No   Can you read, write, and speak simple English?

Yes   No   Do you know about United States government and history?

If you circled **Yes** to all of the questions above, you are ready to apply to become a United States citizen. If you answered **No** to any of the questions above, ask an immigration specialist if you are ready. There are special reasons for answering **No,** and you may still be able to apply to become a U.S. citizen.

☆ THE APPLICATION

You need to submit an application called the N-400 "Application for Naturalization" to the Immigration and Naturalization Service (INS). You also have to submit two photographs of yourself and a check for the application and fingerprint fee (when this book was made, the application fee was $225.00 plus a $25.00 fingerprint fee). The fees may be paid in one check (total of the check is $250.00). Make the check payable to the Immigration and Naturalization Service.

Send These to the INS:
- Form N-400
- Two photographs
- One check for $250.00

You can get the N-400 application from an Immigration and Naturalization Service office near you. Look in Chapter 3 for a list of INS offices. Then you can do one of the following:

- Write them a letter to ask for the form.
- Go to the office and pick up the form.
- Call them on the phone and ask for the form.

You can also get an N-400 application by calling 1-800-870-3676. Tell the truth when you fill out the N-400 application form. Get help if you need it. See Chapter 3 for where to find help.

☆ FINGERPRINTS

Do not send a fingerprint card with your N-400 application. After the INS receives your N-400 application, they will send you an appointment letter with the address of the nearest INS authorized fingerprint site. Read the instructions in the appointment letter. Take the letter to the INS authorized fingerprint site when you go to your fingerprint appointment.

☆ STUDY

Read and study this book and any other material that will help you to understand United States government and history. You need to know the material included in this book. You may want to take a class on how to pass the United States Citizenship Exam.

☆ TAKE A TEST

The INS will test you about United States government and history during your interview. They will ask you questions in English and you will answer them out loud in English. In the future, you may be able to take a written test. During the interview, you will also need to write down one or two sentences that you hear. To pass the test, you must answer 70 percent of the questions correctly. If you do not pass the test, you will get one more try. If you do not pass the test the second time, you will have to start the whole process over and wait another several months to get a new interview date.

> **You can take the test in your native language (not English) if you are:**
> - Fifty-five (55) years old and have lived in America for fifteen (15) years as a lawful Permanent Resident
>
> OR
>
> - Fifty (50) years old and have lived in America for twenty (20) years as a lawful Permanent Resident

☆ THE INTERVIEW

You will be given a date to go for your INS interview. It may take 10–12 months to get a date for the interview. At the interview, you must promise to tell the truth by taking an oath. You will be asked questions about your N-400 application. You will also be asked questions about yourself, your children, your work, and your life. You must answer the questions in English. If you have a physical, mental, or developmental disability, talk to an Immigration Specialist to find out if you can avoid speaking English and answering questions about American government during the interview.

> **You can take an easier test in your native language if you are:**
> - Sixty-five (65) years old and have lived in America for twenty (20) years as a lawful Permanent Resident

SWEARING-IN CEREMONY

If you pass the test and the interview, you will get a letter within two months. The letter will tell you the date and time of a swearing-in ceremony. At the ceremony, you will take the Oath of Allegiance (say that you are loyal to the United States) and exchange your Permanent Residency card for a United States citizenship certificate. After the ceremony, you will be an American citizen.

CITIZENSHIP PROCESS

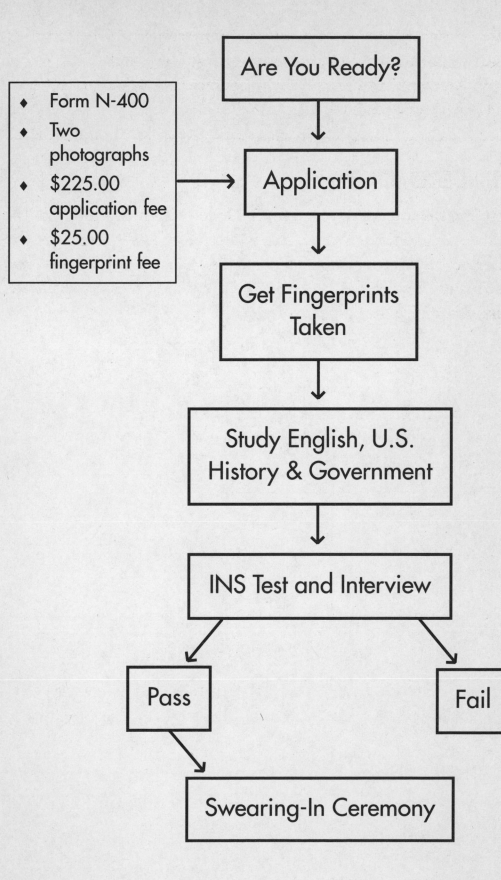

Are You Ready?

- ◆ Form N-400
- ◆ Two photographs
- ◆ $225.00 application fee
- ◆ $25.00 fingerprint fee

Application

Get Fingerprints Taken

Study English, U.S. History & Government

INS Test and Interview

Pass

Fail

Swearing-In Ceremony

CHAPTER 3

How to Get Help

You can find help in becoming a United States citizen in many places. This chapter includes contact information for the four regional Immigration and Naturalization Service (INS) offices so you can find the one for your state. Other groups offer help, too.

☆ INS OFFICE ADDRESSES

Here is a list of where to send your completed N-400 "Application for Naturalization" form. There are four regional INS offices. Look for your state and then send your N-400 application to the address that appears below your state. You can also contact the INS office to get more information about the naturalization process.

North

If you live in one of these states:

Alaska	Michigan	Oregon
Colorado	Minnesota	South Dakota
Idaho	Missouri	Utah
Illinois	Montana	Washington
Indiana	Nebraska	Wisconsin
Iowa	North Dakota	Wyoming
Kansas	Ohio	

Then send your completed N-400 application form to this address:

United States Immigration and Naturalization Service
Nebraska Service Center
Attention N-400 Unit
P.O. Box 87400
Lincoln, NE 68501-7400
(402) 437-5218

West

If you live in one of these states or other areas:

Arizona
California
Commonwealth of the Northern Mariana Islands
Hawaii
Nevada
Territory of Guam

Then send your completed N-400 application form to this address:

United States Immigration and Naturalization Service
California Service Center
Attention N-400 Unit
P.O. Box 10400
Laguna Niguel, CA 92607-0400
(949) 360-2769

South

If you live in one of these states:

Alabama	Louisiana	South Carolina
Arkansas	Mississippi	Tennessee
Florida	New Mexico	Texas
Georgia	North Carolina	
Kentucky	Oklahoma	

Then send your completed N-400 application form to this address:

United States Immigration and Naturalization Service
Texas Service Center
Attention N-400 Unit
P.O. Box 851204
Mesquite, TX 75185-1204
(214) 381-1423

East

If you live in one of these states or other areas:

Commonwealth of Puerto Rico	New Hampshire	Vermont
Connecticut	New Jersey	Virginia
Delaware	New York	Washington, DC
Maine	Pennsylvania	West Virginia
Maryland	Rhode Island	
Massachusetts	U.S. Virgin Islands	

Then send your completed N-400 application form to this address:

United States Immigration and Naturalization Service
Vermont Service Center
Attention N-400 Unit
75 Lower Weldon Street
St. Albans, VT 05479-0001
(802) 527-3160

LEGAL HELP

You may want to pay for an attorney to help you complete the N-400 "Application for Naturalization" form. If so, look in your phone book for the phone number of your state's Bar Association or the Legal Aid Society. Many immigration attorneys also advertise in the yellow pages of the phone book. Be careful when you choose an attorney. Ask friends or relatives to suggest an attorney if they know of a good one.

One place you can write to for more information is the American Immigration Lawyers Association (AILA). It has over 5,200 attorneys who practice immigration law. AILA Member attorneys represent tens of thousands of U.S. families who have applied for permanent residence for their spouses, children, and other close relatives to lawfully enter and reside in the United States. You can ask for a referral to an immigration attorney by contacting them at:

American Immigration Lawyers Association
1400 Eye Street, NW, Suite 1200
Washington, DC 20005
Tel: (202) 216-2400

CHAPTER 4

Citizenship Lessons

Each of the twenty-three lessons in this chapter will help you to pass your citizenship exam. Work slowly and carefully through each lesson, and do all the exercises listed in each lesson.

Here's an outline of what's in this chapter:

LESSON 1

Branches of Government

Three Branches of Government

Judicial | Legislative | Executive

QUESTIONS

Say these questions and answers many times out loud.

1. How many branches are there in the government?

   three (3)

2. What are the three branches of our government?

   executive, legislative, judicial

3. What is the executive branch of our government?

   President, Vice President, Cabinet

4. What is the legislative branch of our government?

   Congress

5. What is the judicial branch of our government?

   Supreme Court

WORDS TO KNOW

branches: separate parts
Congress: people who make our laws
oath: promise to tell the truth

ABOUT THE BRANCHES OF GOVERNMENT

There are three **branches** of government in the United States. The three **branches** are:

1. Executive
2. Legislative
3. Judicial

There are three **branches** of government so that no one branch or person can have too much power. Each **branch** keeps the others from getting too strong. The executive **branch** includes the President, Vice President, and Cabinet. The legislative **branch** includes **Congress**. The judicial **branch** includes the Supreme Court.

Three branches of government

✏ TEST QUESTIONS

Mark your answers to these test questions on the bubble answer sheet below. When you choose an answer choice, fill in the whole circle with a pencil. **Don't** fill in an answer choice like this ◉ or this ✖, but make sure the circle is filled in completely, like this ●. The answers to all the exercises in this lesson begin on page 221.

1. Ⓐ Ⓑ Ⓒ Ⓓ
2. Ⓐ Ⓑ Ⓒ Ⓓ
3. Ⓐ Ⓑ Ⓒ Ⓓ

4. Ⓐ Ⓑ Ⓒ Ⓓ
5. Ⓐ Ⓑ Ⓒ Ⓓ

1. What is the executive branch?
   A. Congress
   B. Supreme Court
   C. President, Vice President, Cabinet
   D. judicial

2. What is the legislative branch?
   A. Congress
   B. Supreme Court
   C. President, Vice President, Cabinet
   D. judicial

3. What is the judicial branch?
   A. Congress
   B. Supreme Court
   C. President, Vice President, Cabinet
   D. judicial

4. What are the three branches of our government?
   A. Congress, President, Cabinet
   B. executive, judicial, legislative
   C. President, Vice President, Cabinet
   D. executive, President, Congress

5. How many branches are there in the government?
   A. one
   B. two
   C. three
   D. four

✎ EXERCISES
Circle the Correct Answer

1.	What is the judicial branch?	Congress	Supreme Court
2.	How many branches of government are there?	five	three
3.	What is the executive branch?	Supreme Court	President, Cabinet, Vice President
4.	What is the legislative branch?	Congress	President
5.	What are the three branches of government?	federal, state, judicial	executive, judicial, legislative

Yes or No Questions

Circle **Yes** if the sentence is true. Circle **No** if the sentence is not true.

Yes   No   The President is in the judicial branch of government.

Yes   No   The Supreme Court is in the judicial branch of government.

Yes   No   There are three branches of government.

Yes   No   The Congress is in the executive branch of government.

Yes   No   The President is in the executive branch of government.

Yes   No   There are five branches of government.

✎ DICTATION PRACTICE

Write each sentence twice. For the first time, you can look at the sentence. For the second time, try writing the sentence without looking.

1. I study.

2. I study English.

3. I study citizenship.

1. _____ .

1. _____ .

2. _____ .

2. _____ .

3. _____ .

3. _____ .

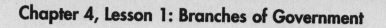 **INTERVIEW PRACTICE**

Here is what you may hear when you begin your interview. Say these phrases out loud several times.

Interviewer:	Please stand and raise your right hand.
What you do:	Get out of your chair and put your right hand in the air.
What does it mean?	You are getting ready to take an **oath**.

Interviewer:	Do you swear that everything you say today will be the truth?
What you do:	Answer out loud, "yes."
What does it mean?	You promise to tell the truth. You promise to tell no lies.

Interviewer:	Do you promise to tell the truth and nothing but the truth, so help you God?
What you do:	Answer out loud, "yes."
What does it mean?	You promise to tell the truth. You promise to tell no lies.

Interviewer:	Please sit down.
What you do:	Get back into your chair.
What does it mean?	The **oath** is finished.

Say these practice questions and answers out loud several times.

Question:	Do you understand what an **oath** is?
Answer:	Yes, it is a promise to tell the truth.

Question: What is your complete name?
Answer: My name is Yolanda Rodriguez Martinez.

Question: What is your name?
Answer: Yolanda Rodriguez Martinez.

Your Turn

Now give your own answers to the interview questions above. Have your partner ask you the question. Then respond with the answer that is correct for you.

LESSON 2

The Legislative Branch

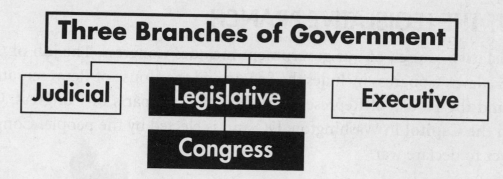

Three Branches of Government

Judicial | Legislative | Executive

Congress

 **QUESTIONS**

Say these questions and answers many times out loud.

1. Who makes the laws in the United States? — Congress

2. What is Congress? — Senate and House of Representatives

3. What are the duties of Congress? — to make laws

4. Who elects Congress? — the people

5. Where does Congress meet? — Capitol in Washington, DC

6. Who has the power to declare war? — Congress

7. What is the United States Capitol? — place where Congress meets

WORDS TO KNOW

legislative branch: Congress
job: work or duty
Capitol: where Congress meets
address: where you live

ABOUT THE LEGISLATIVE BRANCH

The **legislative branch** of our government includes Congress. The **job** of Congress is to make laws. Congress includes the Senate and the House of Representatives. The Senate and the House of Representatives are the two parts of Congress. Congress meets in the **Capitol** in Washington, DC and is elected by the people. Congress has the power to declare war.

Capitol

✏ TEST QUESTIONS

Mark your answers to these test questions on the bubble answer sheet below. When you choose an answer choice, fill in the whole circle with a pencil. **Don't** fill in an answer choice like this ◉ or this ✖, but make sure the circle is filled in completely, like this ●. The answers to all the exercises in this lesson begin on page 222.

1. Ⓐ Ⓑ Ⓒ Ⓓ
2. Ⓐ Ⓑ Ⓒ Ⓓ
3. Ⓐ Ⓑ Ⓒ Ⓓ
4. Ⓐ Ⓑ Ⓒ Ⓓ
5. Ⓐ Ⓑ Ⓒ Ⓓ
6. Ⓐ Ⓑ Ⓒ Ⓓ
7. Ⓐ Ⓑ Ⓒ Ⓓ

1. What does the legislative branch include?
   A. judicial
   B. Supreme Court
   C. President, Vice President, Cabinet
   D. Congress

2. What does Congress do?
   A. elects the mayor
   B. makes laws
   C. interprets laws
   D. collects taxes

3. What are the two parts of Congress?
   A. Senate and Capitol
   B. Senate and Washington, DC
   C. Senate and House of Representatives
   D. House of Representatives and Capitol

4. Where does Congress meet?
   A. in the White House
   B. in the House in New York City
   C. in the House in Philadelphia, Pennsylvania
   D. in the Capitol in Washington, DC

5. Who elects Congress?
   A. the President
   B. the Vice President
   C. the people
   D. the governor of New York

6. What is the United States Capitol?
   A. the place where Congress meets
   B. the President's official residence
   C. the place where the Supreme Court meets
   D. the office of the executive branch

7. Who has the power to declare war?
   A. President
   B. Congress
   C. Supreme Court
   D. Vice President

✐ EXERCISES
Matching Questions

Match the correct answer to each question.

_____Who elects Congress?

_____Who makes the laws in the United States?

_____What is Congress?

_____What are the duties of Congress?

_____Where does Congress meet?

_____What does Congress have the power to declare?

A. the Capitol in Washington, DC

B. to make laws

C. the people

D. Senate and House of Representatives

E. Congress

F. war

Yes or No Questions

Circle **Yes** if the sentence is true. Circle **No** if the sentence is not true.

Yes	No	Congress makes the laws in the United States.
Yes	No	The President has the power to declare war.
Yes	No	Congress includes the Senate and the House of Representatives.
Yes	No	The duties of Congress are to please the people.
Yes	No	The duties of Congress are to make laws.
Yes	No	Congress meets in New York City.
Yes	No	Congress has the power to declare war.

✎ Dictation Practice

Write each sentence twice. For the first time, copy them. For the second time, try to write them without looking.

1. I want to be a citizen.

2. I want to be an American.

1. _____.

1. _____.

2. _____.

2. _____.

👥 INTERVIEW PRACTICE

Say these practice questions and answers out loud several times.

Question: What is your **address?**

Answer: My address is 423 Tenth Avenue, Brooklyn, New York 11209.

Question:	Where do you live?
Answer:	I live at 423 Tenth Avenue, Brooklyn, New York 11209.

Question:	What is your home phone number?
Answer:	My home phone number is 718-555-7889.

Question:	What is your telephone number at home?
Answer:	It is 718-555-7889.

Question:	Do you have a work telephone number?
Answer:	Yes, my work number is 212-555-6000.

Question:	What is your work phone number?
Answer:	My work phone number is 212-555-6000.

Question:	Do you have a work number?
Answer:	No, I am not currently working.

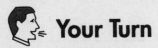 **Your Turn**

Have your partner ask you the interview questions listed above. Then answer the questions out loud.

LESSON 3

Senate

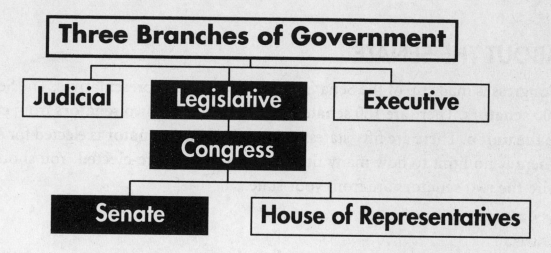

Three Branches of Government

- Judicial
- Legislative
  - Congress
    - Senate
    - House of Representatives
- Executive

 **QUESTIONS**

Say these questions and answers many times out loud.

1. How many senators are there in Congress?   100 (one hundred)

2. Why are there 100 senators in Congress?   two (2) from each state

3. Who are the two senators from your state?   Ask a teacher or a friend for the answer.

4. How long do we elect each senator?   six (6) years

5. How many times can a senator be re-elected?   no limit

WORDS TO KNOW

senators: people who work in the Senate
union: United States of America
re-elected: voted into office again
citizenship: the country where you have the right to fully participate in the benefits and laws of that country

ABOUT THE SENATE

Congress is made up of the Senate and the House of Representatives. The Senate has 100 **senators**. There are 100 **senators** because there are two **senators** from each state in the **union**. There are fifty states in the **union**. Each **senator** is elected for six years. There is no limit to how many times **senators** can be **re-elected**. You should know who the two **senators** are from your state.

Senators

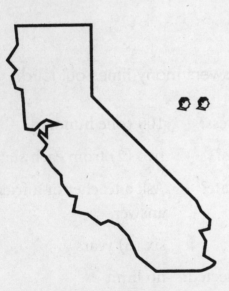

California   Rhode Island

✏ TEST QUESTIONS

Mark your answers to these test questions in the bubble answer sheet below. Make sure you fill in the bubble completely with a pencil. The answers to all the exercises in this lesson begin on page 223.

1. Ⓐ   Ⓑ   Ⓒ   Ⓓ   3. Ⓐ   Ⓑ   Ⓒ   Ⓓ
2. Ⓐ   Ⓑ   Ⓒ   Ⓓ   4. Ⓐ   Ⓑ   Ⓒ   Ⓓ

1. Why are there 100 senators in Congress?
   A. there are 100 states in the union
   B. there are two senators from each state
   C. tradition
   D. because that is all that fits in the Senate Gallery

2. How many times can a senator be re-elected?
   A. zero
   B. one
   C. two
   D. no limit

3. How many senators are in Congress?
   A. 50
   B. 100
   C. 101
   D. 200

4. For how many years is a senator elected?
   A. four
   B. five
   C. six
   D. eight

✎ EXERCISES
Circle the Correct Answer

1.	There are _____ senators in Congress.	100	435
2.	A senator is elected for _____ years.	six	ten
3.	How many times can a senator be re-elected?	no limit	ten
4.	There are 100 senators because there are _____.	two from each state	four from each state
5.	The word "union" means _____.	the United States	provinces in Canada

Yes or No Questions

Circle **Yes** if the sentence is true. Circle **No** if the sentence is not true.

Yes   No   A senator is elected for 100 years.
Yes   No   There are 100 senators because there are two from each state.
Yes   No   There is no limit to how many times a senator can be re-elected.
Yes   No   A senator is elected for six years.
Yes   No   There are 435 senators in Congress.

✎ DICTATION PRACTICE

Write each sentence twice. For the first time, copy the sentences. For the second time, have your partner read the sentences while you write them.

1. I live in California.

2. I live with my family.

3. I live in California with my family.

1. _____.

1. _____.

2. _____.

2. _____.

3. _____.

3. _____.

INTERVIEW PRACTICE

Say these practice questions and answers out loud several times.

Question:	May I see your passport?
Answer:	Yes, here it is.

Question:	Do you have your passport with you?
Answer:	Yes, I do.

Question:	What is your current **citizenship?**
Answer:	I am currently a citizen of Mexico.

Question:	Your current **citizenship** is?
Answer:	Mexican.

Your Turn

Now give your own answers to the interview questions above. Have your partner ask the questions. Then answer them out loud.

LESSON 4

House of Representatives

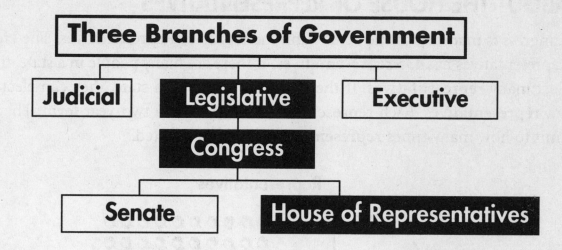

Three Branches of Government

- Judicial
- **Legislative**
  - **Congress**
    - Senate
    - **House of Representatives**
- Executive

 **QUESTIONS**

Say these questions and answers many times out loud.

1. How many representatives are there in Congress? — 435 (four hundred thirty-five)

2. How long do we elect the representatives? — two (2) years

3. How many times can a representative be re-elected? — no limit

4. How many representatives does each state have? — depends on how many people live in the state

WORDS TO KNOW

representatives: people who work in the House of Representatives
term: how long someone works in government
birth place: country where you were born

ABOUT THE HOUSE OF REPRESENTATIVES

Congress is made up of the Senate and the House of Representatives. The House of Representatives has 435 **representatives.** If there are many people in a state, they can elect many **representatives.** If there are few people in a state, they can elect only a few **representatives.** Each **representative** is elected for a two-year **term.** There is no limit to how many times **representatives** can be re-elected.

Representatives

California

✎ TEST QUESTIONS

Mark your answers to these test questions in the bubble answer sheet below. Make sure you fill in the bubble completely with a pencil. The answers to all the exercises in this lesson begin on page 224.

1. Ⓐ Ⓑ Ⓒ Ⓓ   3. Ⓐ Ⓑ Ⓒ Ⓓ
2. Ⓐ Ⓑ Ⓒ Ⓓ   4. Ⓐ Ⓑ Ⓒ Ⓓ

1. How long do we elect the representatives?
   A. one year
   B. two years
   C. three years
   D. four years

2. How many times can a representative be re-elected?
   A. zero
   B. one
   C. two
   D. no limit

3. How many representatives are in Congress?
   A. 100
   B. 101
   C. 435
   D. 450

4. For how many years is a representative elected?
   A. two
   B. four
   C. six
   D. eight

✎ EXERCISES
Fill In the Blanks

1. There are _____ representatives in   435   100
    Congress.

2. A representative is elected for _____ years.   six   two

3. There is _____ to the number of   a limit   no limit
    times a representative can be re-elected.

4. If there are many people in a state, they   many   two
    can elect _____ representatives.

Yes or No Questions

Circle **Yes** if the sentence is true. Circle **No** if the sentence is not true.

Yes   No   A representative is elected for a two-year term.
Yes   No   There are 435 representatives because there are two from each state.
Yes   No   There is no limit to how many times a representative can be
             re-elected.
Yes   No   A representative is elected for two years.
Yes   No   There are 435 representatives in Congress.

✎ DICTATION PRACTICE

Write each sentence twice. For the first time, copy the sentences. For the second
time, try to write the sentences from memory.

1. I want to be an American citizen.

2. I want to be a citizen of the United States.

1. _____.

1. _____.

2. _____.

2. _____.

👥 INTERVIEW PRACTICE

Say these practice questions and answers out loud several times.

Question:	What is your date of birth ?
Answer:	I was born on July 12, 1953.

Question:	When were you born?
Answer:	On July 12, 1953.

Question:	What is your birth date?
Answer:	My birth date is July 12, 1953.

Question:	Where were you born?
Answer:	I was born in India.

Question:	What is your place of birth?
Answer:	I was born in India.

Question:	What is your **birth place?**
Answer:	I was born in India.

👤 Your Turn

Now give your own answers to the interview questions above. Have your partner ask the questions. Then answer them out loud.

ANSWER SHEET FOR REVIEW TESTS

This answer sheet is for review tests 1–6. Cut it out and keep it at the back of your book. Each time you come to a review test, take it out and use it to record your answers. When you choose an answer choice, fill in the whole circle with a pencil. **Don't** fill in an answer choice like this ◉ or this ✖, but make sure the circle is filled in completely, like this ●.

Review Test 1

1. Ⓐ Ⓑ Ⓒ Ⓓ	6. Ⓐ Ⓑ Ⓒ Ⓓ	11. Ⓐ Ⓑ Ⓒ Ⓓ
2. Ⓐ Ⓑ Ⓒ Ⓓ	7. Ⓐ Ⓑ Ⓒ Ⓓ	12. Ⓐ Ⓑ Ⓒ Ⓓ
3. Ⓐ Ⓑ Ⓒ Ⓓ	8. Ⓐ Ⓑ Ⓒ Ⓓ	13. Ⓐ Ⓑ Ⓒ Ⓓ
4. Ⓐ Ⓑ Ⓒ Ⓓ	9. Ⓐ Ⓑ Ⓒ Ⓓ	14. Ⓐ Ⓑ Ⓒ Ⓓ
5. Ⓐ Ⓑ Ⓒ Ⓓ	10. Ⓐ Ⓑ Ⓒ Ⓓ	15. Ⓐ Ⓑ Ⓒ Ⓓ

Review Test 2

1. Ⓐ Ⓑ Ⓒ Ⓓ	6. Ⓐ Ⓑ Ⓒ Ⓓ	11. Ⓐ Ⓑ Ⓒ Ⓓ
2. Ⓐ Ⓑ Ⓒ Ⓓ	7. Ⓐ Ⓑ Ⓒ Ⓓ	12. Ⓐ Ⓑ Ⓒ Ⓓ
3. Ⓐ Ⓑ Ⓒ Ⓓ	8. Ⓐ Ⓑ Ⓒ Ⓓ	13. Ⓐ Ⓑ Ⓒ Ⓓ
4. Ⓐ Ⓑ Ⓒ Ⓓ	9. Ⓐ Ⓑ Ⓒ Ⓓ	14. Ⓐ Ⓑ Ⓒ Ⓓ
5. Ⓐ Ⓑ Ⓒ Ⓓ	10. Ⓐ Ⓑ Ⓒ Ⓓ	

Review Test 3

1. Ⓐ Ⓑ Ⓒ Ⓓ	6. Ⓐ Ⓑ Ⓒ Ⓓ	11. Ⓐ Ⓑ Ⓒ Ⓓ
2. Ⓐ Ⓑ Ⓒ Ⓓ	7. Ⓐ Ⓑ Ⓒ Ⓓ	12. Ⓐ Ⓑ Ⓒ Ⓓ
3. Ⓐ Ⓑ Ⓒ Ⓓ	8. Ⓐ Ⓑ Ⓒ Ⓓ	13. Ⓐ Ⓑ Ⓒ Ⓓ
4. Ⓐ Ⓑ Ⓒ Ⓓ	9. Ⓐ Ⓑ Ⓒ Ⓓ	14. Ⓐ Ⓑ Ⓒ Ⓓ
5. Ⓐ Ⓑ Ⓒ Ⓓ	10. Ⓐ Ⓑ Ⓒ Ⓓ	15. Ⓐ Ⓑ Ⓒ Ⓓ

Review Test 4

1. Ⓐ Ⓑ Ⓒ Ⓓ	6. Ⓐ Ⓑ Ⓒ Ⓓ	11. Ⓐ Ⓑ Ⓒ Ⓓ
2. Ⓐ Ⓑ Ⓒ Ⓓ	7. Ⓐ Ⓑ Ⓒ Ⓓ	12. Ⓐ Ⓑ Ⓒ Ⓓ
3. Ⓐ Ⓑ Ⓒ Ⓓ	8. Ⓐ Ⓑ Ⓒ Ⓓ	
4. Ⓐ Ⓑ Ⓒ Ⓓ	9. Ⓐ Ⓑ Ⓒ Ⓓ	
5. Ⓐ Ⓑ Ⓒ Ⓓ	10. Ⓐ Ⓑ Ⓒ Ⓓ	

Review Test 5

1. (A)   (B)   (C)   (D)   6. (A)   (B)   (C)   (D)
2. (A)   (B)   (C)   (D)   7. (A)   (B)   (C)   (D)
3. (A)   (B)   (C)   (D)   8. (A)   (B)   (C)   (D)
4. (A)   (B)   (C)   (D)   9. (A)   (B)   (C)   (D)
5. (A)   (B)   (C)   (D)

Review Test 6

1. (A)   (B)   (C)   (D)   6. (A)   (B)   (C)   (D)   11. (A)   (B)   (C)   (D)
2. (A)   (B)   (C)   (D)   7. (A)   (B)   (C)   (D)   12. (A)   (B)   (C)   (D)
3. (A)   (B)   (C)   (D)   8. (A)   (B)   (C)   (D)   13. (A)   (B)   (C)   (D)
4. (A)   (B)   (C)   (D)   9. (A)   (B)   (C)   (D)   14. (A)   (B)   (C)   (D)
5. (A)   (B)   (C)   (D)   10. (A)   (B)   (C)   (D)   15. (A)   (B)   (C)   (D)

REVIEW TEST 1

Mark your answers to these test questions on the bubble answer sheet on page 39. The answers to this test are given on page 224.

1. How many branches of the government are there?
A. one
B. two
C. three
D. four

2. What is the legislative branch?
A. Congress
B. Supreme Court
C. President
D. mayor

3. What is the judicial branch?
A. Congress
B. President
C. Vice President
D. Supreme Court

4. What is the executive branch?
   A. President, Vice President, Cabinet
   B. Congress
   C. Supreme Court
   D. House of Representatives

5. What are the three branches of government?
   A. Supreme Court, President, Congress
   B. executive, legislative, judicial
   C. Senate, House of Representatives, Cabinet
   D. law, federal, Congress

6. Where does Congress meet?
   A. Supreme Court
   B. Capitol in Washington, DC
   C. New York City
   D. White House

7. What is Congress?
   A. President
   B. Senate and House of Representatives
   C. Senate and Supreme Court
   D. governor

8. Who elects Congress?
   A. Electoral College
   B. President
   C. mayor
   D. the people

9. Who makes the laws in the United States?
   A. Supreme Court
   B. President
   C. Congress
   D. mayor

10. What is the job of Congress?
  A. to make laws
  B. to enforce laws
  C. to interpret laws
  D. to collect money

11. Why are there 100 senators in Congress?
  A. two from each state
  B. four from each state
  C. six from each state
  D. seven from each state

12. How many times can a senator be re-elected?
  A. two
  B. four
  C. no limit
  D. five

13. How long do we elect each senator?
  A. three years
  B. two years
  C. six years
  D. four years

14. How many senators are there in Congress?
  A. 100
  B. 435
  C. 600
  D. 50

15. How many representatives are there in Congress?
  A. 100
  B. 435
  C. 600
  D. 50

LESSON 5

The Judicial Branch

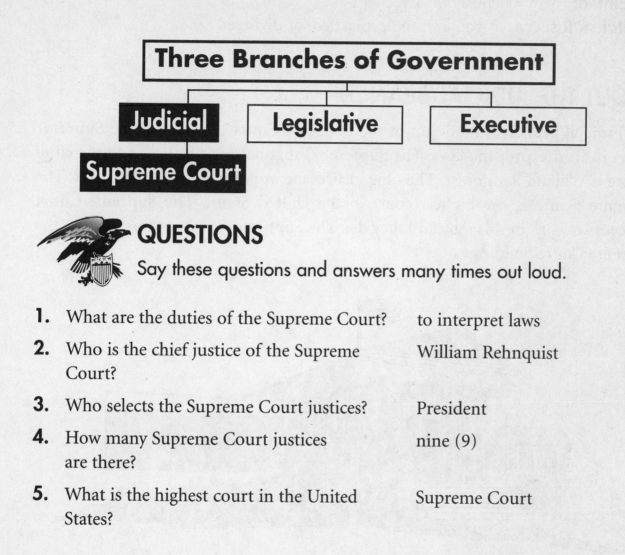

Three Branches of Government

Judicial — Legislative — Executive

Supreme Court

QUESTIONS

Say these questions and answers many times out loud.

1. What are the duties of the Supreme Court?   to interpret laws

2. Who is the chief justice of the Supreme Court?   William Rehnquist

3. Who selects the Supreme Court justices?   President

4. How many Supreme Court justices are there?   nine (9)

5. What is the highest court in the United States?   Supreme Court

WORDS TO KNOW

judicial branch:	the part of the government that includes the Supreme Court
Supreme Court:	highest court in the United States
interpret:	to explain
chief justice:	head of the Supreme Court
appointed:	chosen or selected
marital status:	if you are single, married, or divorced

ABOUT THE JUDICIAL BRANCH

The **judicial branch** is made up of the **Supreme Court**. The job of the **Supreme Court** is to **interpret** the laws. The **Supreme Court** has nine justices and the **chief justice** is William Rehnquist. The nine justices are **appointed** by the President. The **Supreme Court** is the highest court in the United States. The **Supreme Court** justices can work in this job until they die. The **Supreme Court** justices work in the **Supreme Court** building.

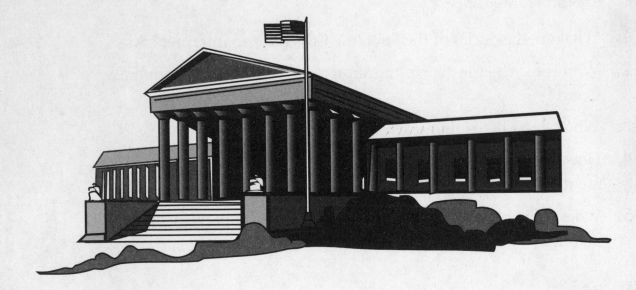

✎ TEST QUESTIONS

Mark your answers to these test questions in the bubble answer sheet below. Make sure you fill in the bubble completely with a pencil. The answers to all the exercises in this lesson begin on page 225.

1. Ⓐ Ⓑ Ⓒ Ⓓ   4. Ⓐ Ⓑ Ⓒ Ⓓ
2. Ⓐ Ⓑ Ⓒ Ⓓ   5. Ⓐ Ⓑ Ⓒ Ⓓ
3. Ⓐ Ⓑ Ⓒ Ⓓ

1. How many Supreme Court justices are there?
   A. eight
   B. nine
   C. ten
   D. eleven

2. Who appoints the Supreme Court justices?
   A. the people
   B. Congress
   C. the President
   D. the Vice President

3. What is the job of the Supreme Court justices?
   A. to make laws
   B. to collect money
   C. to interpret laws
   D. to entertain the public

4. Who is the chief justice of the Supreme Court?
   A. Bill Clinton
   B. Al Gore
   C. Judge Judy
   D. William Rehnquist

5. What is the highest court in the United States?
   A. Supreme Court
   B. Judges Court
   C. White House
   D. Capitol

✏ EXERCISES
Fill In the Blanks

1. The _____ selects the Supreme Court justices.   President   Cabinet

2. The duty of the Supreme Court is to _____ laws.   interpret   make

3. The _____ Court is the highest court in the United States.   State   Supreme

4. There are _____ justices on the Supreme Court.   ten   nine

5. William _____ is the chief justice of the Supreme Court.   Gore   Rehnquist

Yes or No Questions

Circle **Yes** if the sentence is true. Circle **No** if the sentence is not true.

Yes	No	The duty of the Supreme Court is to make laws.
Yes	No	The duty of the Supreme Court is to interpret laws.
Yes	No	There are nine justices on the Supreme Court.
Yes	No	William Rehnquist is the Vice President.
Yes	No	The President appoints the Supreme Court justices.

✏ DICTATION PRACTICE

Write each sentence twice. For the first time, copy the sentences. For the second time, try to write the sentences from memory.

1. I drive to work.

2. I drive my car to work.

3. I like to drive my car to work.

1. _____.

1. _____.

2. _____.

2. _____.

3. _____.

3. _____.

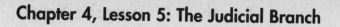 **INTERVIEW PRACTICE**

Say these practice questions and answers out loud several times.

Question: What is your **marital status?**
Answer: I am married.

Question: What is your **marital status?**
Answer: I am divorced.

Question: Are you married?
Answer: No, I am single.

Question: Have you ever been married previously?
Answer: Yes, I was married for one year when I lived in Mexico.

Question: Is your husband a United States citizen?
Answer: No, he is not a United States citizen.

Question: Is your wife a United States citizen?
Answer: Yes, she is.

Question: Why did you get a divorce?
Answer: We fought too much.

Question: How long have you been married?
Answer: I have been married for ten years.

Your Turn

Now give your own answers to the interview questions above. Have your partner ask the questions. Then answer them out loud.

LESSON 6

The Executive Branch

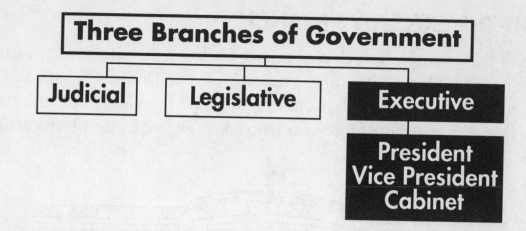

Three Branches of Government

Judicial   Legislative   Executive

President
Vice President
Cabinet

QUESTIONS

Say these questions and answers many times out loud.

1. What is the job of the executive branch? — to enforce the law

2. Who was the first President of the United States? — George Washington

3. Who is the President of the United States today? — Bill Clinton

4. Who is the Vice President today? — Al Gore

5. Who elects the President of the United States? — the Electoral College

6. How long do we elect the President? — four (4) years

WORDS TO KNOW

executive branch: part of government made up of the President, Vice President, and Cabinet

Electoral College: group who elects the President

port of entry: place where you arrived in the country

ABOUT THE EXECUTIVE BRANCH

The job of the **executive branch** is to enforce the law. It includes the President, Vice President, and Cabinet. The first President of the United States was George Washington. The President today is Bill Clinton, and the Vice President is Al Gore. The President is elected for a four-year term and is elected by the **Electoral College**.

White House

/ TEST QUESTIONS

Mark your answers to these test questions in the bubble answer sheet below. Make sure you fill in the bubble completely with a pencil. The answers to all the exercises in this lesson begin on page 225.

1. Ⓐ   Ⓑ   Ⓒ   Ⓓ
2. Ⓐ   Ⓑ   Ⓒ   Ⓓ
3. Ⓐ   Ⓑ   Ⓒ   Ⓓ

4. Ⓐ   Ⓑ   Ⓒ   Ⓓ
5. Ⓐ   Ⓑ   Ⓒ   Ⓓ

1. Who elects the President of the United States?
   A. Senate
   B. Congress
   C. Electoral College
   D. Cabinet

2. Who was the first President of the United States?
   A. Bill Clinton
   B. William Rehnquist
   C. Abraham Lincoln
   D. George Washington

3. What is the duty of the executive branch?
   A. to enforce laws
   B. to interpret laws
   C. to collect money
   D. to buy land

4. How long do we elect the President?
   A. one year
   B. two years
   C. three years
   D. four years

5. Who is the Vice President today?
   A. Al Gore
   B. Bill Clinton
   C. William Rehnquist
   D. George Washington

✎ EXERCISES

Matching Questions

Match the correct answer to each question.

_____first President of the United States

_____Vice President

_____how long the President is elected

_____President today

_____elects the President

_____duty of executive branch

A. four years

B. Bill Clinton

C. Electoral College

D. Al Gore

E. George Washington

F. enforce the law

Yes or No Questions

Circle **Yes** if the sentence is true. Circle **No** if the sentence is not true.

Yes	No	The duty of the executive branch is to enforce laws.
Yes	No	The duty of the executive branch is to interpret laws.
Yes	No	George Washington was the first President of the United States.
Yes	No	Bill Clinton is the Vice President today.
Yes	No	The President is elected by the Electoral College.
Yes	No	The President is elected for four years.

✎ DICTATION PRACTICE

Write each sentence twice. For the first time, copy the sentences. For the second time, have your partner read the sentences to you while you write without looking.

1. I take the bus.

2. I take the bus to work.

3. I like to take the bus.

1. _____.

1. _____.

2. _____.

2. _____.

3. _____.

3. _____.

INTERVIEW PRACTICE

Say these practice questions and answers out loud several times.

Question: How long have you been a Permanent Resident of the United States?
Answer: I have been a resident for ten years.

Question: When did you first come to the United States?
Answer: I arrived in the United States in 1989.

Question: On what date did you enter the United States?
Answer: I arrived in the United States on September 5, 1989.

Question: How long have you lived in the United States?
Answer: I have lived in the United States for ten years.

Question: Where did you enter the United States?
Answer: I entered the United States in New York City.

Question: What was your **port of entry?**
Answer: JFK airport in New York City.

Question: In what **port of entry** did you arrive in America?
Answer: My port of entry was the Los Angeles airport.

Question: What was your **port of entry?**
Answer: I crossed the United States border near Seattle, Washington.

Question: When did you become a Permanent Resident?
Answer: I became a Permanent Rresident in 1990.

Question: In what year did you arrive in the United States?
Answer: I came to America in 1989.

Your Turn

Now give your own answers to the interview questions above. Have your partner ask the questions. Then answer them out loud.

LESSON 7

Office of the President

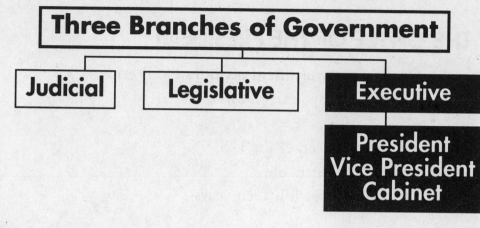

Three Branches of Government

- Judicial
- Legislative
- Executive
  - President
  - Vice President
  - Cabinet

 **QUESTIONS**

Say these questions and answers many times out loud.

1. Who becomes President of the United States if the President dies?

   Vice President

2. How many terms can a President serve?

   two (2)

3. Who becomes President of the United States if the President and Vice President die?

   Speaker of the House of Representatives

4. What are the requirements to be President?

   natural born citizen of the U.S., thirty-five (35) years old, lived in the U.S. fourteen (14) years

5. What special group advises the President?

   Cabinet

WORDS TO KNOW

Cabinet: fourteen people who help the President make decisions
natural born citizen: person who is born in a country
advises: gives help to
employer: the name of the company or person you work for
occupation: the name of your job

ABOUT THE OFFICE OF THE PRESIDENT

The executive branch of the government includes the President, Vice President, and **Cabinet**. To become President, you need to:

- be a **natural born citizen** of the U.S.
- be at least thirty-five years old
- have lived in the U.S. for fourteen years

The **Cabinet** is a special group of people that **advises** the President. The President can serve two terms. If the President dies, the Vice President becomes President. If both the President and the Vice President die, then the Speaker of the House of Representatives becomes President.

President

✏ TEST QUESTIONS

Mark your answers to these test questions in the bubble answer sheet below. Make sure you fill in the bubble completely with a pencil. The answers to all the exercises in this lesson begin on page 226.

1. Ⓐ   Ⓑ   Ⓒ   Ⓓ   4. Ⓐ   Ⓑ   Ⓒ   Ⓓ
2. Ⓐ   Ⓑ   Ⓒ   Ⓓ   5. Ⓐ   Ⓑ   Ⓒ   Ⓓ
3. Ⓐ   Ⓑ   Ⓒ   Ⓓ

1. A President can serve how many terms?
   A. one
   B. two
   C. three
   D. four

2. Who becomes the President if the President dies?
   A. Vice President
   B. First Lady
   C. a Cabinet member
   D. the Supreme Court Justice

3. What special group advises the President?
   A. Congress
   B. Supreme Court
   C. taxpayers
   D. Cabinet

4. Who becomes President if both the President and the Vice President die?
   A. spouse of the President
   B. chief justice of the Supreme Court
   C. the Senate Majority Leader
   D. Speaker of the House of Representatives

5. What is one requirement to be President?
   A. born in Europe
   B. thirty-five years old
   C. lived in the United States for five years
   D. speak Latin

✎ EXERCISES
Circle the Correct Answer

1. What is one requirement to be President?   born in Canada   natural born citizen of the U.S.

2. Who becomes President if the President dies?   First Lady   Vice President

3. What special group advises the President?   Congress   Cabinet

4. Who becomes President if the President and Vice President die   Speaker of the House of Representatives   Congress

   Representatives

5. How many terms can a President serve?   two   three

Yes or No Questions

Circle **Yes** if the sentence is true. Circle **No** if the sentence is not true.

Yes   No   To become President, you must be a natural born citizen of the U.S.
Yes   No   The Cabinet advises the President.
Yes   No   The duty of the executive branch is to enforce laws.
Yes   No   The First Lady becomes President if the President dies.
Yes   No   The executive branch of the government includes the President, Vice President, and Cabinet.
Yes   No   The President can serve two terms in office.
Yes   No   To become President, you must be at least fifty years old.

✎ DICTATION PRACTICE

Write each sentence twice. Then have your partner read the sentences to you. Write each sentence as you hear it on the next page.

1. I go to school.
2. My children go to school.
3. My children and I go to school.

1. _____.

1. _____.

2. _____.

2. _____.

3. _____.

3. _____.

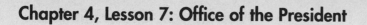 **INTERVIEW PRACTICE**

Say these practice questions and answers out loud several times.

Question:	Who is your **employer?**
Answer:	I am unemployed right now.

Question:	Why aren't you working?
Answer:	I was laid off from my last job, and I'm looking for a new job.

Question:	Who is your current **employer?**
Answer:	My employer is Machines, Inc.

Question:	Who do you currently work for?
Answer:	I work for Machines, Inc.

Question:	Are you currently working?
Answer:	Yes, I work for Machines, Inc.

Question:	What kind of work do you do?
Answer:	I work for Machines, Inc. as a factory worker.

Question:　　　　Do you have a job?
Answer:　　　　　Yes, I work at Machines, Inc.

Question:　　　　What is your **occupation?**
Answer:　　　　　I am a factory worker.

Question:　　　　What kind of income do you have?
Answer:　　　　　I get an income from working for Machines, Inc.

Question:　　　　How do you support yourself?
Answer:　　　　　I work for Machines, Inc.

Question:　　　　How long have you held this job?
Answer:　　　　　I have had this job for three years.

Question:　　　　Who was your **employer** before that?
Answer:　　　　　I used to work for Southwest Airlines.

Question:　　　　What job did you have there?
Answer:　　　　　I worked as a shipping clerk.

Your Turn

Now give your own answer. Have your partner ask you the interview questions above. Respond with the answers that are correct for you.

REVIEW TEST 2

Mark your answers to these test questions in the bubble answer sheet on page 39. Make sure you fill in the bubble completely with a pencil. The answers to this test are given on page 227.

1. How many times can a representative be re-elected?
   A. one
   B. two
   C. three
   D. no limit

2. How long do we elect the representatives?
   A. two years
   B. three years
   C. four years
   D. five years

3. How many representatives are there in Congress?
   A. 435
   B. 100
   C. 2
   D. 500

4. What are the duties of the Supreme Court?
   A. enforce the laws
   B. make laws
   C. interpret laws
   D. declare war

5. Who is the chief justice of the Supreme Court?
   A. William Rehnquist
   B. Bill Clinton
   C. Al Gore
   D. Janet Reno

6. Who selects the Supreme Court justices?
   A. President
   B. Congress
   C. Vice President
   D. Supreme Court

7. How many Supreme Court justices are there?
   A. one
   B. five
   C. seven
   D. nine

8. What is the highest court in the United States?
   A. Supreme Court
   B. Federal Court
   C. City Court
   D. State Court

9. How long do we elect the President?
   A. two years
   B. six years
   C. four years
   D. three years

10. Who elects the President?

    A. Congress

    B. Electoral College

    C. Supreme Court

    D. mayor

11. Who is the Vice President today?

    A. Bill Clinton

    B. Al Gore

    C. George Bush

    D. Henry Kissinger

12. Who is the President of the United States today?

    A. Bill Clinton

    B. Tony Major

    C. William Rehnquist

    D. Al Gore

13. Who was the first President of the United States?

    A. Thomas Jefferson

    B. Bill Clinton

    C. George Washington

    D. Abraham Lincoln

14. What is the job of the executive branch?

    A. make laws

    B. interpret laws

    C. enforce laws

    D. vote

LESSON 8

More About the President

President
- White House
- Voted for in November
- Inaugurated in January

 ## QUESTIONS

Say these questions and answers many times out loud.

1. What is the White House? — President's official home

2. Where is the White House located? — Washington, DC

3. In what month do we vote for the President? — November

4. In what month is the new President inaugurated? — January

5. What is the name of the President's official home? — White House

WORDS TO KNOW

inaugurated: sworn into office
White House: place where the President lives while serving as President
born: when a baby comes into the world

ABOUT THE PRESIDENT

The President is the head executive of the United States. We vote for the President in November. Then, in January, the new President is **inaugurated**. During the President's term of office, the President lives in the **White House** in Washington, DC.

Vote in November

President inaugurated in January

✏ TEST QUESTIONS

Mark your answers to these test questions in the bubble answer sheet below. Make sure you fill in the bubble completely with a pencil. The answers to all the exercises in this lesson begin on page 227.

1. Ⓐ   Ⓑ   Ⓒ   Ⓓ   4. Ⓐ   Ⓑ   Ⓒ   Ⓓ
2. Ⓐ   Ⓑ   Ⓒ   Ⓓ   5. Ⓐ   Ⓑ   Ⓒ   Ⓓ
3. Ⓐ   Ⓑ   Ⓒ   Ⓓ

1. We vote for the President in which month?
   A. October
   B. November
   C. December
   D. January

2. The President is inaugurated in which month?
   A. October
   B. November
   C. December
   D. January

3. What is the President's official home called?
   A. Capitol
   B. White House
   C. Supreme Court
   D. Oval Office

4. Where is the White House located?
   A. Washington, DC
   B. New York, NY
   C. Los Angeles, CA
   D. Philadelphia, PA

5. What happens in November?
   A. the President is inaugurated
   B. our taxes are due
   C. we vote for the President
   D. the President moves into the White House

✎ EXERCISES
Matching Questions

Match the correct answer to each question.

_____the President's official home	A. January
_____we vote for the President during this month	B. White House
_____the President is inaugurated during this month	C. Washington, DC
_____the White House is located here	D. November

Yes or No Questions

Circle **Yes** if the sentence is true. Circle **No** if the sentence is not true.

Yes	No	The White House is located in Philadelphia, PA.
Yes	No	The White House is the President's official home.
Yes	No	The President is inaugurated in November.
Yes	No	We vote for the President in January.
Yes	No	The Cabinet is the President's official home.
Yes	No	The White House is located in Washington, DC.
Yes	No	The President is inaugurated in January.
Yes	No	We vote for the President in November.

✎ DICTATION PRACTICE

Write each sentence twice. First practice copying the sentences. Then have your partner read the sentences while you write without looking.

1. The little girl is happy.
2. My family is happy to be in America.
3. The little girl and my family are happy.

1. _____ .

1. _____ .

2. _____ .

2. _____ .

3. _____ .

3. _____ .

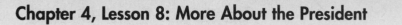 ## INTERVIEW PRACTICE

Say these practice questions and answers out loud several times.

Question:	How many children do you have?
Answer:	I have three children.

Question:	Do your children live with you?
Answer:	Yes, my children live in my home.

Question:	How many people live in your house?
Answer:	Five people: myself, my husband, and three children.

Question:	Who do you live with?
Answer:	I live with my husband and three children.

Question:	Where do your children live?
Answer:	My children live with me in Brooklyn, New York.

Question:	Did any of your children stay in your native country?
Answer:	No, all of my children live with me here in Brooklyn.

Question: When were your children **born?**
Answer: One was born in 1992, one in 1994, and one in 1997.

Question: Were they all **born** in the United States?
Answer: Yes, they were born in America.

Your Turn

Now give your own answers to the interview questions above. Have your partner ask you the question. Then respond with the answer that is correct for you.

LESSON 9

Head Executives

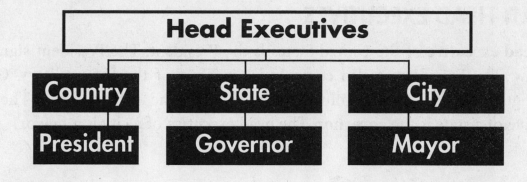

Head Executives

Country	State	City
President	Governor	Mayor

 ## QUESTIONS

Say these questions and answers many times out loud.

1. What is the head executive of a state government called? governor

2. What is the head executive of a city government called? mayor

3. Who signs bills into law? President

4. Who is commander in chief of the U.S. military? President

5. Who was the first commander in chief of the U.S. military? George Washington

WORDS TO KNOW

head executive: the leader or person in charge
governor: leader of a state
mayor: leader of a city
deported: a judge in court ordered you to go back to your first country

ABOUT HEAD EXECUTIVES

The **head executive** of the United States is the President. The President signs bills into law. The President is also commander in chief of the U.S. military. George Washington was the first commander in chief of the U.S. military. The head executive of a state is the **governor**. The head executive of a city is a **mayor**.

The President leads the country.

A governor leads a state.

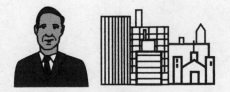

A mayor leads a city.

╱ TEST QUESTIONS

Mark your answers to these test questions in the bubble answer sheet below. Make sure you fill in the bubble completely with a pencil. The answers to all the exercises in this lesson begin on page 228.

1. Ⓐ   Ⓑ   Ⓒ   Ⓓ   4. Ⓐ   Ⓑ   Ⓒ   Ⓓ
2. Ⓐ   Ⓑ   Ⓒ   Ⓓ   5. Ⓐ   Ⓑ   Ⓒ   Ⓓ
3. Ⓐ   Ⓑ   Ⓒ   Ⓓ

1. Who signs bills into law?
   A. President
   B. Vice President
   C. Speaker of the House
   D. Congress

2. Who was the first commander in chief of the U.S. military?
   A. Bill Clinton
   B. William Rehnquist
   C. Abraham Lincoln
   D. George Washington

3. What is the head of a city government called?
   A. President
   B. governor
   C. mayor
   D. Cabinet

4. What is the head of a state government called?
   A. President
   B. governor
   C. mayor
   D. Cabinet

5. Who is commander in chief of the U.S. military?
   A. Al Gore
   B. Bill Clinton
   C. William Rehnquist
   D. George Washington

✎ EXERCISES
Fill In the Blanks

1. The _____ signs a bill into law.   Congress   President

2. The head executive of a city government is   governor   mayor
   the _____.

3. The _____ is commander in chief   President   citizen
   of the U.S. military.

4. The _____ is head executive of a state   President   governor
   government.

5. The first commander in chief of the U.S.   George   Al Gore
   military was _____.   Washington

Yes or No Questions

Circle **Yes** if the sentence is true. Circle **No** if the sentence is not true.

Yes No   The governor is the head executive of a city government.
Yes No   The President signs a bill into law.
Yes No   George Washington was the first commander in chief of the U.S.
          military.
Yes No   The mayor is the head executive of a city government.
Yes No   Bill Clinton is the commander in chief of the U.S. military today.
Yes No   The President is the head executive of the United States.
Yes No   The mayor is the head executive of a state government.

✎ DICTATION PRACTICE

Read each sentence once, try to remember it, and then write it again.

1. I believe in freedom.

2. I believe in the Constitution.

3. I believe in freedom and the Constitution.

1. _____.

1. _____.

2. _____.

2. _____.

3. _____.

3. _____.

INTERVIEW PRACTICE

Say these practice questions and answers out loud several times.

Question: How many times have you left the United States since you became a Permanent Resident?

Answer: I went out of America only one time.

Question: How long were you away?

Answer: I was gone for three weeks.

Question: Where did you go?

Answer: I went to visit my aunt in Poland.

Question: Why did you leave the United States?

Answer: I wanted to visit my aunt in Poland because she was dying.

Question: Since becoming a Permanent Resident, have you ever left the United States?

Answer: I left only once to go visit my grandmother in Mexico.

Question: When was the last time you left the United States?

Answer: I went to Canada two years ago.

Question: Have you left the United States since you became a Permanent Resident?

Answer: No, I've never left the United States.

Question: Since coming to the U.S., have you traveled to any other country?

Answer: No, I've never left the United States.

Question: Have you visited any other country since becoming a Permanent Resident?

Answer: Yes, I went to Poland to visit my aunt one time.

Question: Have you ever been **deported** by the Immigration office?

Answer: No, I have never been ordered to leave America.

Question: Were you ever ordered to leave the United States?

Answer: No, I have never been **deported**.

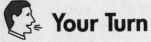 **Your Turn**

Now give your own answers to the interview questions above. Have your partner ask the questions. Then answer them out loud.

REVIEW TEST 3

Mark your answers to these test questions in the bubble answer sheet on page 39. Make sure you fill in the bubble completely with a pencil. The answers to this test are given on page 229.

1. Who becomes President if the President and Vice President die?
   A. Congress
   B. Supreme Court justice
   C. Speaker of the House of Representatives
   D. governor

2. How many terms can a President serve?
   A. two
   B. three
   C. one
   D. no limit

3. Who becomes President of the U.S. if the President dies?
   A. Vice President
   B. Speaker of the House of Representatives
   C. mayor
   D. senator

4. What is one requirement to be President?
    A. natural born citizen of the U.S.
    B. lived in Canada
    C. be male
    D. speak Spanish

5. What special group advises the President?
    A. Congress
    B. Cabinet
    C. Parliament
    D. Supreme Court

6. Who was the first commander in chief of the U.S. military?
    A. Thomas Jefferson
    B. Bill Clinton
    C. George Bush
    D. George Washington

7. Who is commander in chief of the U.S. military?
    A. Al Gore
    B. Bill Clinton
    C. George Washington
    D. Abraham Lincoln

8. What is the President's official home?
    A. White House
    B. New York
    C. Gray House
    D. Brown House

9. Who signs bills into law?
    A. Congress
    B. Supreme Court
    C. Vice President
    D. President

10. What is the head executive of a city government called?
  A. mayor
  B. governor
  C. President
  D. senator

11. What is the head executive of a state government called?
  A. President
  B. mayor
  C. governor
  D. Supreme Court justice

12. What is the White House?
  A. where Congress meets
  B. President's official home
  C. governor's home
  D. where Supreme Court meets

13. Where is the White House located?
  A. Washington, DC
  B. New York
  C. Los Angeles
  D. Chicago

14. In what month do we vote for President?
  A. October
  B. January
  C. December
  D. November

15. In what month is the President inaugurated?
  A. March
  B. April
  C. September
  D. January

LESSON 10

The Constitution

Constitution	
Supreme Law of the Land	Changes Are Amendments

 **QUESTIONS**

Say these questions and answers many times out loud.

1. What is the Constitution? — the supreme law of the land

2. Can the Constitution be changed? — yes

3. What do we call changes to the Constitution? — amendments

4. How many amendments are there? — twenty-seven (27)

5. What is the supreme law of the United States? — Constitution

6. When was the Constitution written? — 1787

WORDS TO KNOW

Constitution: the supreme law of the United States
amendments: changes
different: another
maiden name: a woman's last name before getting married

ABOUT THE CONSTITUTION

The supreme law of the land is the **Constitution**. It begins with the words, "We the people of the United States." It was written in 1787. It can be changed. Changes to the **Constitution** are called **amendments**. There have been twenty-seven **amendments** to the **Constitution**.

We the People *of the United States,*

in order to form a more perfect union, establish justice, insure domestic tranquility,

provide for the common defense, promote the general welfare, and secure the blessings

of liberty to ourselves and our posterity, do ordain and establish this Constitution

for the United States of America.

Article I

The Constitution

✎ TEST QUESTIONS

Mark your answers to these test questions in the bubble answer sheet below. Make sure you fill in the bubble completely with a pencil. The answers to all the exercises in this lesson begin on page 229.

1. Ⓐ Ⓑ Ⓒ Ⓓ   4. Ⓐ Ⓑ Ⓒ Ⓓ
2. Ⓐ Ⓑ Ⓒ Ⓓ   5. Ⓐ Ⓑ Ⓒ Ⓓ
3. Ⓐ Ⓑ Ⓒ Ⓓ

1. What is the supreme law of the land?
  A. President
  B. Cabinet
  C. Constitution
  D. Capitol

2. What is a change to the Constitution called?
  A. assurance
  B. amendment
  C. addition
  D. deletion

3. When was the Constitution written?
  A. 1998
  B. 1787
  C. 1776
  D. 1800

4. What is the Constitution?
  A. the supreme law of the land
  B. an award-winning book
  C. the Supreme Court
  D. the executive branch

5. How many amendments to the Constitution are there?
  A. twenty-four
  B. twenty-five
  C. twenty-six
  D. twenty-seven

✏ EXERCISES
Fill In the Blanks

1. There are _____ amendments to the Constitution.	twenty-four	twenty-seven
2. A change to the Constitution is an _____.	amendment	appeal
3. The Constitution is the supreme _____ of the land.	law	crime
4. _____, the Constitution can be changed.	No	Yes
5. The supreme law of the land is the _____.	Constitution	Congress
6. The Constitution was written in _____.	1787	1785

Yes or No Questions

Circle **Yes** if the sentence is true. Circle **No** if the sentence is not true.

Yes	No	The Constitution is the supreme law of the land.
Yes	No	A change to the Constitution is called an amendment.
Yes	No	The Constitution cannot be changed.
Yes	No	The Constitution was written in 1776.
Yes	No	The supreme law of the land is the Constitution.
Yes	No	There are twenty-seven amendments to the Constitution.
Yes	No	The Constitution was written in 1787.
Yes	No	There are twenty-four amendments to the Constitution.

✏ DICTATION PRACTICE

Write each sentence twice. For the first time, copy the sentences. For the second time, have your partner read the sentences while you write them.

1. The sky is blue.

2. My dog is brown.

3. The sky is blue and my dog is brown.

1. _____ .

1. _____ .

2. _____ .

2. _____ .

3. _____ .

3. _____ .

INTERVIEW PRACTICE

Say these practice questions and answers out loud several times.

Question:	Have you ever used a **different** name?
Answer:	Yes, my last name used to be Alloutuseth.
Question:	Do you want to change your name?
Answer:	Yes, I want to change my last name to Allseth.
Question:	What other names have you gone by?
Answer:	I used to be called Massouleh Alloutuseth.
Question:	To what do you want to change your name?
Answer:	I want my new name to be Sue Allseth.

Question: What name do you want to have now?
Answer: Sue Allseth.

Question: How do you spell that?
Answer: S-u-e A-l-l-s-e-t-h.

Question: What other names have you used in the past?
Answer: I've never used any other names.

Question: What was your **maiden name?**
Answer: Before I was married, my name was Massouleh Tomei.

Question: What other names have you used in the past?
Answer: Before I was married my name was Massouleh Tomei.

Question: When did you change your name?
Answer: I changed my name ten years ago when I was married.

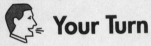 **Your Turn**

Now give your own answers to the interview questions above. Have your partner ask the questions. Then answer them out loud.

LESSON 11

More About the Constitution

Constitution

Supreme Law of the Land	Bill of Rights

 ## QUESTIONS

Say these questions and answers many times out loud.

1. What is the Bill of Rights? — the first ten amendments

2. Where does the freedom of speech come from? — the Bill of Rights

3. What are the first ten amendments called? — the Bill of Rights

4. Whose rights are guaranteed by the Constitution and the Bill of Rights? — everyone in America, including non-citizens

5. What is the introduction to the Constitution called? — the preamble

WORDS TO KNOW

introduction: the beginning
preamble: the introduction to the Constitution
arrested: formally charged by a police officer
crime: breaking the law

ABOUT THE CONSTITUTION

The Constitution is the supreme law of the land. The **introduction** to the Constitution is called the **preamble**. The first ten amendments to the Constitution are called the Bill of Rights. One of the amendments in the Bill of Rights grants freedom of speech. Everyone in America is protected by the Constitution and the Bill of Rights, including non-citizens.

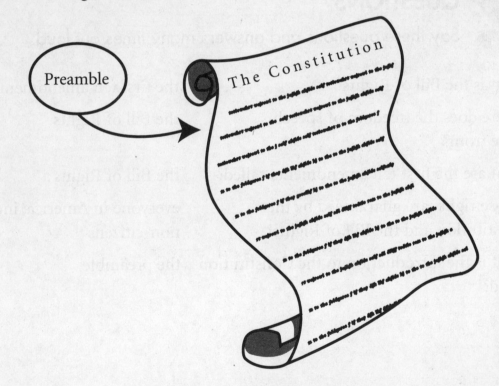

✎ TEST QUESTIONS

Mark your answers to these test questions in the bubble answer sheet below. Make sure you fill in the bubble completely with a pencil. The answers to all the exercises in this lesson begin on page 230.

1. Ⓐ　Ⓑ　Ⓒ　Ⓓ　　　4. Ⓐ　Ⓑ　Ⓒ　Ⓓ
2. Ⓐ　Ⓑ　Ⓒ　Ⓓ　　　5. Ⓐ　Ⓑ　Ⓒ　Ⓓ
3. Ⓐ　Ⓑ　Ⓒ　Ⓓ

1. What are the first ten amendments to the Constitution called?
   A. preamble
   B. introduction
   C. Bill of Rights
   D. Book of Law

2. What is the Bill of Rights?
   A. last ten amendments to the Constitution
   B. changes to the Declaration of Statehood
   C. additions to the President's speech
   D. first ten amendments to the Constitution

3. Where does freedom of speech come from?
   A. Bill of Rights
   B. President
   C. Pilgrims
   D. Supreme Court

4. Whose rights are guaranteed by the Constitution?
   A. Canadians
   B. Europeans
   C. American citizens only
   D. everyone in America, including non-citizens

5. What is the introduction to the Constitution called?
   A. preamble
   B. epilogue
   C. beginning
   D. story

✒ EXERCISES
Circle the Correct Answer

1.	the first ten amendments	Bill of Rights	Congress
2.	the introduction to the Constitution	preamble	Bill of Rights
3.	freedom of speech comes from here	President	Bill of Rights
4.	the Constitution guarantees these people rights	only citizens	everyone
5.	the Bill of Rights	first ten amendments	Supreme Court

Yes or No Questions

Circle **Yes** if the sentence is true. Circle **No** if the sentence is not true.

Yes	No	The Constitution is the supreme law of the land.
Yes	No	The first ten amendments to the Constitution are called the Bill of Rights.
Yes	No	Freedom of speech comes from the Bill of Rights.
Yes	No	The Bill of Rights is the first twelve amendments to the Constitution.
Yes	No	The introduction to the Constitution is called the preamble.
Yes	No	Everyone is protected by the Bill of Rights, including non-citizens.
Yes	No	The Bill of Rights is the first ten amendments to the Constitution.
Yes	No	The conclusion to the Constitution is called the preamble.

✒ DICTATION PRACTICE

Write each sentence twice. Then have your partner read the sentences to you. Write each sentence as you hear it on a different piece of paper.

1. There is a bird.
2. The bird is in the tree.
3. There is a bird in the tree.

1. _____ .

1. _____ .

2. _____ .

2. _____ .

3. _____ .

3. _____ .

 **INTERVIEW PRACTICE**

Say these practice questions and answers out loud several times.

Question:　Why do you want to be an American citizen?
Answer:　I want to vote.

Question:　Why do you want to be a U.S. citizen?
Answer:　I want to travel with a U.S. passport.

Question:　Why have you applied for naturalization?
Answer:　I want to bring my mother to America.

Question:　Were you ever **arrested?**
Answer:　Yes, a long time ago.

Question:　What were you **arrested** for?
Answer:　I stole some money from the corner store.

Question:　How about any other arrests?
Answer:　No, that was the only time I was arrested.

Question: Have you ever committed any **crime** for which you have not been **arrested?**

Answer: No, I've never done any crimes that I wasn't punished for.

Question: Have you ever been imprisoned for breaking any law?

Answer: I was in jail for three months for robbing the corner store.

Question: When was that?

Answer: During the winter of 1989.

Your Turn

Now give your own answers to the interview questions above. Have your partner ask the questions. Then answer them out loud.

LESSON 12

Bill of Rights

Constitution		
Bill of Rights	**=**	**First Ten Amendments**

QUESTIONS

Say these questions and answers many times out loud.

1. What are the first ten amendments?   Bill of Rights

2. What are the freedoms guaranteed by the Bill of Rights?

    1. The freedom of speech, press, and religion

    2. Right to bear arms

    3. Government may not put soldiers in people's homes

    4. Government may not search or take a person's property without a warrant

    5. A person may not be tried for the samecrime twice

    6. A person charged with a crime has rights including the right to a trial and a lawyer

    7. People are protected from unreasonable fines or cruel punishment

3. Name one right guaranteed by the first amendment.

    freedom of: speech, press, religion, peaceable assembly, and requesting change of government

WORDS TO KNOW

Bill of Rights: first ten amendments
bear arms: carry a gun
income tax: the money you pay to the government if you work in America
warrant: official permission from a judge
tried: put through a trial with a judge and jury

ABOUT THE BILL OF RIGHTS

The Constitution is the supreme law of the land. The first ten amendments to the Constitution are called the **Bill of Rights**. Everyone in the United States is protected by the **Bill of Rights**, including non-citizens. Some of the **Bill of Rights** include:

1.   The freedom of speech, press, and religion
2.   Right to **bear arms**
3.   Government may not put soldiers in people's homes
4.   Government may not search or take a person's property without a **warrant**
5.   A person may not be **tried** for the same crime twice
6.   A person charged with a crime has rights including the right to a trial and a lawyer
7.   People are protected from unreasonable fines or cruel punishment

✏️ TEST QUESTIONS

Mark your answers to these test questions in the bubble answer sheet below. Make sure you fill in the bubble completely with a pencil. The answers to all the exercises in this lesson begin on page 231.

1. Ⓐ Ⓑ Ⓒ Ⓓ
2. Ⓐ Ⓑ Ⓒ Ⓓ
3. Ⓐ Ⓑ Ⓒ Ⓓ
4. Ⓐ Ⓑ Ⓒ Ⓓ
5. Ⓐ Ⓑ Ⓒ Ⓓ

1. What are the first ten amendments to the Constitution called?
   A. preamble
   B. introduction
   C. Bill of Rights
   D. Book of Law

2. Which freedom is guaranteed by the Bill of Rights?
   A. right to pay taxes
   B. right to bear arms
   C. right to get paid for your work
   D. right to govern your neighbor

3. Which freedom is guaranteed by the Bill of Rights?
   A. government may put soldiers in people's homes
   B. government may search anyone without a warrant
   C. government may not enter contests
   D. government may not put soldiers in people's homes

4. Which freedom is guaranteed by the Bill of Rights?
   A. a person may not be tried for the same crime twice
   B. a person may walk on the moon
   C. a person may kill his or her neighbor
   D. a person charged with a crime may not get a trial

5. Which freedom is guaranteed by the Bill of Rights?
   A. freedom to steal from your neighbor
   B. freedom of speech
   C. freedom to fight the government
   D. freedom to set off a bomb

✎ EXERCISES

List the Correct Answers
What are the freedoms guaranteed by the Bill of Rights?

1. _____

2. _____

3. _____

4. _____

5. _____

6. _____

7. _____

Yes or No Questions

Circle **Yes** if the sentence is true. Circle **No** if the sentence is not true.

Yes	No	The Constitution is the supreme law of the land.
Yes	No	The first ten amendments to the Constitution are called the Bill of Rights.
Yes	No	Freedom of speech comes from the Bill of Rights.
Yes	No	The right to bear arms comes from the Bill of Rights.
Yes	No	Everyone is protected by the Bill of Rights, including non-citizens.
Yes	No	The government may not search or take a person's property without a warrant.
Yes	No	The Bill of Rights is the first ten amendments to the Constitution.
Yes	No	A person in America may not be tried for the same crime twice.
Yes	No	People in America are not protected from unreasonable fines.
Yes	No	Freedom of religion comes from the Bill of Rights.
Yes	No	The government may not put soldiers in people's homes.

✏ DICTATION PRACTICE

Write each sentence twice. For the first time, copy the sentence. For the second time, try to write the sentence from memory.

1. I have four children.
2. I live with my children.
3. I live with my four children.

1. _____.

1. _____.

2. _____.

2. _____.

3. _____.

3. _____.

🗣 INTERVIEW PRACTICE

Say these practice questions and answers out loud several times.

Question: Have you ever failed to file a federal **income tax** return?
Answer: No, I have always filed my taxes.

Question: Have you filed your federal taxes every year?
Answer: Yes, I pay my taxes every year.

Question: Do you pay taxes?
Answer: Yes, I pay federal and state taxes each year.

Question: Was there ever a year when you didn't file your federal tax forms?
Answer: No, I've filed my tax forms every year since I came to America.

Question: Was there ever a year when you didn't file your federal tax forms?
Answer: Yes, I didn't file my first two years in America because I made no money.

Question: Do you pay taxes?
Answer: No, I don't have a job so I don't pay federal income taxes.

Your Turn

Now give your own answers to the interview questions above. Have your partner ask the questions. Then answer them out loud.

REVIEW TEST 4

Mark your answers to these test questions in the bubble answer sheet on page 39. Make sure you fill in the bubble completely with a pencil. The answers to this test are given on page 232.

1. When was the Constitution written?
   A. 1787
   B. 1789
   C. 1777
   D. 1749

2. What is the supreme law of the United States?
   A. Declaration of Independence
   B. Constitution
   C. Supreme Court
   D. Congress

3. How many amendments are there?
   A. twenty-three
   B. twenty-five
   C. twenty-six
   D. twenty-seven

4. What do we call a change to the Constitution?
  A. amendment
  B. objection
  C. law
  D. President

5. Can the Constitution be changed?
  A. no
  B. yes

6. What is the Constitution?
  A. supreme law of the land
  B. Congress
  C. Supreme Court
  D. Declaration of Independence

7. What are the first ten amendments called?
  A. supreme law
  B. Constitution
  C. Bill of Rights
  D. citizen rights

8. Whose rights are guaranteed by the Constitution?
  A. only citizens
  B. only the President
  C. only Congress
  D. both citizens and non-citizens

9. What is the introduction to the Constitution called?
  A. Bill of Rights
  B. supreme law of the land
  C. preface
  D. preamble

10. Where does the freedom of speech come from?
  A. President
  B. Congress
  C. Bill of Rights
  D. Supreme Court

11. What is the Bill of Rights?
    A. first ten amendments
    B. Declaration of Independence
    C. code of ethics
    D. code of good works

12. What is one right guaranteed by the Bill of Rights?
    A. freedom of speech
    B. freedom to fight the government
    C. freedom to kill your neighbor
    D. freedom to rob your neighbor

LESSON 13
Pilgrims

 ## QUESTIONS

Say these questions and answers many times out loud.

1. Why did the pilgrims come to America?   religious freedom

2. Who helped the pilgrims in America?   Native Americans

3. What ship brought the pilgrims to America?   Mayflower

4. What holiday was celebrated for the first time by the American colonists?   Thanksgiving

5. Who were the first American colonists?   pilgrims

WORDS TO KNOW

pilgrims:	people who came to America on a ship called the Mayflower
Native Americans:	people who lived in America when the pilgrims arrived
habitual drunkard:	person who drinks too much alcohol
polygamy:	having more than one husband or one wife at the same time
prostitute:	to sell your body for money

ABOUT THE PILGRIMS

The **pilgrims** came to America for religious freedom. The **pilgrims** were the first American colonists. When they came to America, they met the **Native Americans**. The **Native Americans** helped the **pilgrims**. The **pilgrims** came to America on a ship called the Mayflower. In America, the first holiday the **pilgrims** celebrated was Thanksgiving. They celebrated it with the **Native Americans**.

Pilgrims

✎ TEST QUESTIONS

Mark your answers to these test questions in the bubble answer sheet below. Make sure you fill in the bubble completely with a pencil. The answers to all the exercises in this lesson begin on page 232.

1. Ⓐ Ⓑ Ⓒ Ⓓ　　　4. Ⓐ Ⓑ Ⓒ Ⓓ
2. Ⓐ Ⓑ Ⓒ Ⓓ　　　5. Ⓐ Ⓑ Ⓒ Ⓓ
3. Ⓐ Ⓑ Ⓒ Ⓓ

1. Who did the pilgrims meet when they came to America?
   A. Native Americans
   B. Europeans
   C. Canadians
   D. judges

2. Why did the pilgrims come to America?
   A. chance to get rich
   B. hope for new homes
   C. religious freedom
   D. to leave their relatives

3. What ship brought the pilgrims to America?
   A. Red Rose
   B. Mayday
   C. Flower
   D. Mayflower

4. What holiday did the pilgrims celebrate with the Native Americans?
   A. Thanksgiving
   B. Halloween
   C. Easter
   D. Valentine's Day

5. Who helped the pilgrims when they arrived in America?
   A. animals
   B. Native Americans
   C. Mexicans
   D. Chinese

✎ EXERCISES
Matching Questions

Match the correct answer to each question.

_____ship that brought the pilgrims to America   A. Thanksgiving

_____helped the pilgrims in America   B. religious freedom

_____holiday celebrated by the American   C. Native Americans
       colonists

_____reason pilgrims came to America   D. Mayflower

Yes or No Questions

Circle **Yes** if the sentence is true. Circle **No** if the sentence is not true.

Yes	No	The Native Americans helped the pilgrims.
Yes	No	The pilgrims came to America because they wanted a vacation.
Yes	No	The pilgrims came to America on a ship called the Titanic.
Yes	No	Thanksgiving was the first holiday celebrated by the pilgrims.
Yes	No	The pilgrims were the first American colonists.
Yes	No	The pilgrims came to America for religious freedom.
Yes	No	Easter was the first holiday celebrated by the pilgrims.
Yes	No	A ship called the Mayflower brought the pilgrims to America.

✎ DICTATION PRACTICE

Write each sentence twice. For the first time, copy the sentence. For the second time, have your partner read the sentence while you write it.

1. I drive a car.

2. I drive a big red car.

3. I like my car.

1. _____ .

1. _____ .

2. _____ .

2. _____ .

3. _____ .

3. _____ .

INTERVIEW PRACTICE

Say these practice questions and answers out loud several times.

Question:	Have you ever been a **habitual drunkard?**
Answer:	No, I don't drink alcohol.

Question:	Have you ever been a **habitual drunkard?**
Answer:	No, I drink only a little.

Question:	Were you ever drunk every day?
Answer:	No, I drink only one glass of wine a week.

Question:	Have you ever advocated or practiced **polygamy?**
Answer:	No, I have only one wife.

Question:	Have you ever been married to more than one person at a time?
Answer:	No, I have always had only one husband.

Question:	Have you ever practiced **polygamy?**
Answer:	No, I am not married, and I have never been married.

Question: Have you ever been a **prostitute?**
Answer: No, I don't sell my body.

Question: Have you ever been a **prostitute?**
Answer: No, I've never taken money for sex.

Question: Have you ever sold your body for money?
Answer: No, I've never been a **prostitute.**

👤 Your Turn

Now give your own answers to the interview questions above. Have your partner ask the questions. Then answer them out loud.

LESSON 14

Colonies

Colonies
Original 13 States

 **QUESTIONS**

Say these questions and answers many times out loud.

1. What are the thirteen original states called?   colonies

2. Can you name the original thirteen states?

1. Connecticut
2. New Hampshire
3. New York
4. New Jersey
5. Massachusetts
6. Pennsylvania
7. Delaware
8. Virginia
9. North Carolina
10. South Carolina
11. Georgia
12. Rhode Island
13. Maryland

handwritten notes:
3 New H Y J
2 corboline N & S
1 C connecticut
1 D Delaware
1 P Pennsylvania
1 G Georgia
2 M Maryland
    Massachusetts
1 R Rhode Island
1 V virginia

3 H&V
2 M
2 corbois
1 P   C
1 D   D
1 C   G
1 G   P
1 R   R
1 V   V

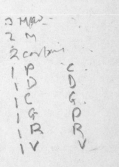

WORDS TO KNOW

colonies: original thirteen states in America
smuggle: illegally sneaking someone or something into the country
illegal drugs: narcotics, cocaine, marijuana, dope, speed
illegal gambling: to play cards for money at someone's house

ABOUT THE COLONIES

The thirteen original states were called the **colonies**. The original thirteen **colonies** were Connecticut, New Hampshire, New York, New Jersey, Massachusetts, Pennsylvania, Delaware, Virginia, North Carolina, South Carolina, Georgia, Rhode Island, and Maryland. The **colonies** were ruled by the king of England, King George.

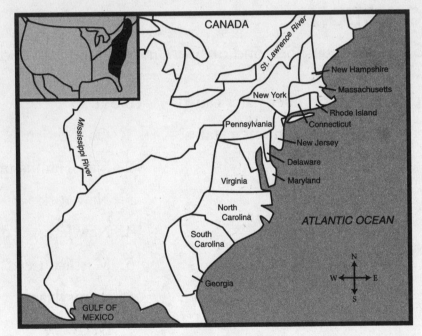

The thirteen colonies

✏ TEST QUESTIONS

Mark your answers to these test questions in the bubble answer sheet below. Make sure you fill in the bubble completely with a pencil. The answers to all the exercises in this lesson begin on page 233.

1. Ⓐ Ⓑ Ⓒ Ⓓ
2. Ⓐ Ⓑ Ⓒ Ⓓ
3. Ⓐ Ⓑ Ⓒ Ⓓ

4. Ⓐ Ⓑ Ⓒ Ⓓ
5. Ⓐ Ⓑ Ⓒ Ⓓ

1. What were the thirteen original states called?
   A. Native American cities
   B. colonies
   C. states
   D. settlements

2. Which state was a part of the thirteen colonies?
   A. Connecticut
   B. California
   C. Washington
   D. Nevada

3. Which state was a part of the thirteen colonies?
   A. Texas
   B. New York
   C. California
   D. Minnesota

4. Which state was a part of the thirteen colonies?
   A. Virginia
   B. California
   C. Texas
   D. Oregon

5. Which state was a part of the thirteen colonies?
   A. Maryland
   B. California
   C. Wisconsin
   D. Texas

✎ EXERCISES
Fill In the Blanks

1. The original thirteen states were called   colonies   provinces
   the _____.

2. Name two of the original thirteen states: Connecticut/   Texas/
   _____ and _____.   New Hampshire   Montana

3. Name two more of the original thirteen   California/   New York/
   states: _____ and _____. Utah   New Jersey

Yes or No Questions

Circle **Yes** if the sentence is true. Circle **No** if the sentence is not true.

Yes	No	The thirteen original states were called the colonies.
Yes	No	New York was one of the colonies.
Yes	No	Texas was one of the colonies.
Yes	No	The thirteen original states were called the settlements.
Yes	No	Connecticut was one of the original thirteen states.
Yes	No	California was one of the original thirteen states.
Yes	No	Georgia was one of the colonies.
Yes	No	Maryland was one of the original thirteen states.

✎ DICTATION PRACTICE

Write each sentence twice. For the first time, copy the sentence. For the second time, have your partner read the sentence while you write.

1. I live in a house.
2. I live in a blue house.
3. I like my house.

1. _____.

1. _____.

2. _____.

2. _____.

3. _____.

3. _____.

INTERVIEW PRACTICE

Say these practice questions and answers out loud several times.

Question: Have you ever knowingly and for gain helped any alien to enter the U.S. illegally?

Answer: No, I have never **smuggled** anyone into the country.

Question: Have you ever helped someone enter the U.S. illegally?

Answer: No, I have never **smuggled** anyone into the country.

Question: Have you ever **smuggled** anyone into the U.S.?

Answer: No, I have never helped anyone enter America illegally.

Question: Have you ever accepted money for sneaking someone into the U.S.?

Answer: No, I have never helped anyone enter America illegally.

Question: Have you ever been a trafficker in **illegal drugs?**

Answer: No, I have never touched illegal drugs.

Question: Have you ever bought or sold **illegal drugs?**

Answer: No, I am not a drug trafficker.

Question: Have you ever carried **illegal drugs** for someone else?

Answer: No, I have never handled illegal drugs.

Question: Have you ever been a trafficker in cocaine or crack?
Answer: No, I have never sold or carried drugs.

Question: Have you ever bought or sold marijuana or speed?
Answer: No, I have never purchased or sold illegal drugs.

Question: Have you ever received income from **illegal gambling?**
Answer: No, I don't gamble.

Question: Did you ever get money illegally from gambling?
Answer: No, I don't play cards for money.

Question: Have you ever received money from **illegal gambling?**
Answer: No, I don't play cards in anyone's house.

Question: Have you ever received money or other goods from **illegal gambling?**
Answer: No, I don't bet on anything.

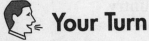 **Your Turn**

Now give your own answers to the interview questions above. Have your partner ask the questions. Then answer them out loud.

LESSON 15

Declaration of Independence

Declaration of Independence

All Men Are Created Equal

 QUESTIONS

Say these questions and answers many times out loud.

1. What is the 4th of July? — Independence Day

2. When was the Declaration of Independence adopted? — July 4, 1776

3. What is the basic belief of the Declaration of Independence? — All men are created equal.

4. Who was the main writer of the Declaration of Independence? — Thomas Jefferson

5. What is the date of Independence Day? — July 4th

WORDS TO KNOW

Declaration of Independence: written statement saying the colonies wanted to
                                    be free from England

basic belief: main idea, most important part

adopted: put into effect

Independence Day: July 4th

claimed: said something was true; pretended

registered: officially signed up to do something

ABOUT THE COLONIES

The colonies were not happy being ruled by England. So Thomas Jefferson wrote the **Declaration of Independence**. The Declaration said that the colonies wanted to be free from England. The **basic belief** of the **Declaration of Independence** is that all men are created equal. The **Declaration of Independence** was **adopted** on July 4, 1776. July 4th in the United States is **Independence Day**.

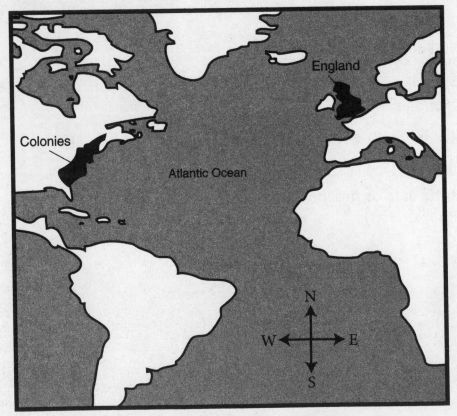

Colonies seek freedom from England

✎ TEST QUESTIONS

Mark your answers to these test questions in the bubble answer sheet below. Make sure you fill in the bubble completely with a pencil. The answers to all the exercises in this lesson begin on page 234.

1. Ⓐ Ⓑ Ⓒ Ⓓ   4. Ⓐ Ⓑ Ⓒ Ⓓ
2. Ⓐ Ⓑ Ⓒ Ⓓ   5. Ⓐ Ⓑ Ⓒ Ⓓ
3. Ⓐ Ⓑ Ⓒ Ⓓ

1. When was the Declaration of Independence adopted?
   A. 1776
   B. 1777
   C. 1789
   D. 1787

2. What is the basic belief of the Declaration of Independence?
   A. all men should fight in an army
   B. all men are created equal
   C. the President has absolute power
   D. only citizens can live in America

3. Who was the main writer of the Declaration of Independence?
   A. Abraham Lincoln
   B. Bill Clinton
   C. Thomas Jefferson
   D. George Washington

4. What is the date of Independence Day?
   A. June 4th
   B. December 25th
   C. July 1st
   D. July 4th

5. What is the 4th of July?
   A. Memorial Day
   B. Valentine's Day
   C. Veteran's Day
   D. Independence Day

SIGNING THE DECLARATION OF INDEPENDENCE

✎ EXERCISES
Fill In the Blanks

1. The Declaration of Independence was adopted on _____, 1776.   July 4   December 25

2. The basic belief of the Declaration of Independence is _____.   America comes first   all men are created equal

3. _____ Day is on the 4th of July.   Independence   Memorial

4. The main writer of the Declaration of Independence was _____.   George Washington   Thomas Jefferson

5. Independence Day is on July _____.   10th   4th

Yes or No Questions

Circle **Yes** if the sentence is true. Circle **No** if the sentence is not true.

Yes   No   The 4th of July is Independence Day.

Yes   No   The basic belief of the Declaration of Independence is that all men are created equal.

Yes   No   The Declaration of Independence was adopted in 1776.

Yes   No   The main writer of the Declaration of Independence was George Washington.

Yes   No   The basic belief of the Declaration of Independence is that the people should work seven days a week.

Yes   No   The Declaration of Independence was written in 1787.

Yes   No   The basic belief of the Declaration of Independence is that the President should have absolute power.

Yes   No   The Declaration of Independence was adopted on July 4, 1776.

Yes   No   The main writer of the Declaration of Independence was Thomas Jefferson.

Yes   No   Independence Day is on December 25th.

✎ DICTATION PRACTICE

Write each sentence twice. For the first time, copy the sentence. For the second time, try to write the sentence from memory.

1. The woman eats.

2. The woman eats food.

3. The woman eats two apples.

1. _____.

1. _____.

2. _____.

2. _____.

3. _____.

3. _____.

👥 INTERVIEW PRACTICE

Say these practice questions and answers out loud several times.

Question: Have you ever **claimed** in writing or in any other way to be a U.S. citizen?

Answer: No, I have never lied about my status.

Question: Have you ever **claimed** in writing or in any other way to be a U.S. citizen?

Answer: No, I never said I was a U.S. citizen.

Question: Have you ever pretended to be a U.S. citizen?
Answer: No, I have never lied about my citizenship.

Question: Have you ever **claimed** in writing to be a U.S. citizen?
Answer: No, I have never pretended to be an American citizen.

Question: Have you ever **claimed** in writing or in any other way to be a U.S. citizen?
Answer: No, I am not a U.S. citizen.

Question: Have you ever voted or **registered** to vote in the United States?
Answer: No, I have never tried to vote because I am not a U.S. citizen.

Question: Have you ever voted or **registered** to vote in the United States?
Answer: No, I am not a U.S. citizen.

Question: Have you ever voted or **registered** to vote in the United States?
Answer: No, I have never tried to vote in America.

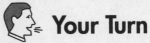 **Your Turn**

Now give your own answers to the interview questions above. Have your partner ask the questions. Then answer them out loud.

REVIEW TEST 5

Mark your answers to these test questions in the bubble answer sheet on page 40. Make sure you fill in the bubble completely with a pencil. The answers to this test are given on page 235.

1. Why did the pilgrims come to America?
    A. to pay taxes
    B. religious freedom
    C. farm land
    D. to escape war

2. What ship brought the pilgrims to America?
    A. Maine
    B. Nina
    C. Mayflower
    D. Pinta

3. What holiday was first celebrated by the American colonists?
    A. Christmas
    B. Halloween
    C. New Year's
    D. Thanksgiving

4. Who helped the pilgrims in America?

A. Native Americans

B. colonists

C. slaves

D. President

5. Who was the main writer of the Declaration of Independence?

A. George Washington

B. Bill Clinton

C. Abraham Lincoln

D. Thomas Jefferson

6. When was the Declaration of Independence written?

A. July 4, 1778

B. July 4, 1776

C. July 4, 1777

D. July 4, 1771

7. What is the basic belief of the Declaration of Independence?

A. the President has absolute power

B. only citizens can vote

C. all men are created equal

D. only citizens can live in the United States

8. What were the thirteen original states called?

A. colonies

B. territories

C. provinces

D. settlements

9. Which one was a colony?

A. California

B. Washington

C. Minnesota

D. New York

LESSON 16

Revolutionary War and George Washington

Revolutionary War	
George Washington	Father of Our Country

 **QUESTIONS**

Say these questions and answers many times out loud.

1. Which President was the first commander in chief of the U.S. military?　George Washington

2. Who did the United States gain independence from?　England

3. What country did we fight during the Revolutionary War?　England

4. Who was the first President elected by the people in the United States?　George Washington

5. Who said, "Give me liberty or give me death"?　Patrick Henry

6. Which President is called the "father of our country"?　George Washington

WORDS TO KNOW

Revolutionary War: war between the thirteen colonies and England
independence: freedom
liberty: freedom
Oath of Allegiance: officially swear to help the United States

ABOUT THE REVOLUTIONARY WAR AND GEORGE WASHINGTON

During the **Revolutionary War,** the United States fought England to gain **independence**. Patrick Henry said, "Give me **liberty** or give me death." The colonists were led by the first commander in chief of the U.S. military, George Washington. The United States gained **independence** from England. After the **Revolutionary War,** George Washington was the first President elected by the people in the United States. He is called the "father of our country."

George Washington

✏ TEST QUESTIONS

Mark your answers to these test questions in the bubble answer sheet below. Make sure you fill in the bubble completely with a pencil. The answers to all the exercises in this lesson begin on page 235.

1. Ⓐ Ⓑ Ⓒ Ⓓ   4. Ⓐ Ⓑ Ⓒ Ⓓ
2. Ⓐ Ⓑ Ⓒ Ⓓ   5. Ⓐ Ⓑ Ⓒ Ⓓ
3. Ⓐ Ⓑ Ⓒ Ⓓ   6. Ⓐ Ⓑ Ⓒ Ⓓ

1. Who did the United States gain independence from?
  A. England
  B. France
  C. Spain
  D. Mexico

2. Who is called the "father of our country"?
  A. Abraham Lincoln
  B. George Washington
  C. Bill Clinton
  D. Thomas Jefferson

3. Which President was the first commander in chief of the U.S. military?
  A. Bill Clinton
  B. Abraham Lincoln
  C. George Washington
  D. Thomas Jefferson

4. Who said, "Give me liberty or give me death"?
  A. George Washington
  B. Patrick Henry
  C. Thomas Jefferson
  D. Abraham Lincoln

5. Who was the first President elected by the people in the United States?
  A. George Washington
  B. Abraham Lincoln
  C. Thomas Jefferson
  D. John Adams

6. What country did we fight during the Revolutionary War?
   A. Spain
   B. France
   C. England
   D. Russia

✎ EXERCISES
Fill In the Blanks

1. _____ was the first commander   George   Thomas
   in chief of the U.S. military.   Washington   Jefferson

2. Patrick _____ said, "Give me liberty   Washington   Henry
   or give me death."

3. The U.S. gained independence from   England   France
   _____.

4. The United States fought _____   England   France
   during the Revolutionary War.

5. _____ was the first President   George   Thomas
   elected by the people in the United States.   Washington   Jefferson

6. George Washington is called the "father of   country   state
   our _____."

Yes or No Questions

Circle **Yes** if the sentence is true. Circle **No** if the sentence is not true.

Yes   **No**   George Washington was the first commander in chief of the U.S. military.

Yes   **No**   America fought France during the Revolutionary War.

Yes   **No**   Thomas Jefferson said, "Give me liberty or give me death."

Yes   **No**   The U.S. gained independence from England.

Yes   **No**   George Washington is called the "father of our country."

Yes   **No**   Patrick Henry said, "Give me life or freedom."

Yes   **No**   America fought England during the Revolutionary War.

Yes   No   Patrick Henry said, "Give me liberty or give me death."

Yes   No   George Washington was the first President elected by the people in the United States.

✏ DICTATION PRACTICE

Write each sentence twice. For the first time, copy the sentence. For the second time, have your partner read the sentence while you write it.

1. I have a cat.

2. I have a small cat.

3. I like cats.

1. _____.

1. _____.

2. _____.

2. _____.

3. _____.

3. _____.

🗣 INTERVIEW PRACTICE

Say these practice questions and answers out loud several times.

Question: Do you believe in the Constitution and the government of the United States?

Answer: Yes, I think the Constitution is a good law.

Question: Do you believe in the Constitution of the United States?
Answer: Yes, I want to follow the Constitution.

Question: Do you believe in the government of the United States?
Answer: Yes, I think the government is very good.

Question: Do you believe in the Constitution and the government of the United States?
Answer: Yes, I believe that the Constitution is a good law.

Question: Are you willing to take the full **Oath of Allegiance** to the United States?
Answer: Yes, I am ready to help my new country.

Question: Are you willing to take the full **Oath of Allegiance** to the United States?
Answer: Yes, I promise to help my new country. I can't help my old country.

Question: Are you willing to take the full **Oath of Allegiance** to the United States?
Answer: Yes, I want to do what is best for America.

Question: Are you willing to take the full **Oath of Allegiance** to the United States?
Answer: Yes, I want to officially swear to help the United States.

Your Turn

Now give your own answers to the interview questions above. Have your partner ask the questions. Then answer them out loud.

LESSON 17

Civil War

```
                    Civil War

    North against South       North Won the War
```

 ## QUESTIONS

Say these questions and answers many times out loud.

1. What was one of the reasons for the Civil War?   slavery

2. Who wanted to start their own country?   the South

3. Who wanted the states to stay together?   the North

4. Who fought during the Civil War?   the North and South

5. Who won the Civil War?   the North

R

WORDS TO KNOW

Civil War: war between the North and South
slave: someone who is owned by another person
incompetent: mind does not work (crazy)
mental institution: hospital for people whose minds don't work
nobility: family is king or queen or is related to them
persecution: hurt someone because of their race, religion, national origin,
                           or political opinion

ABOUT THE CIVIL WAR

In the 1860s, a war began between states in the North and states in the South. It was
called the **Civil War** because it was fought between states in the same country.
Several states in the South wanted to start their own country. They didn't want to be
a part of the United States. The North wanted all the states to stay together but
without slavery. One reason for the **Civil War** was slavery. Many people in the South
owned **slaves**. Many people in the North were against slavery. The North won the
war.

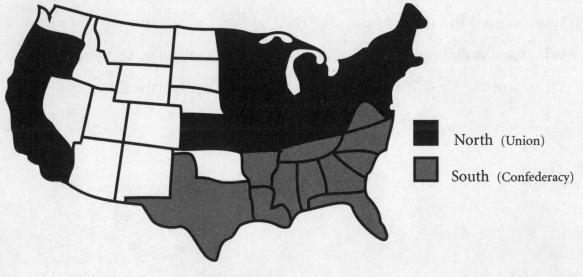

■ North (Union)

■ South (Confederacy)

The Civil War

✏ TEST QUESTIONS

Mark your answers to these test questions in the bubble answer sheet below. Make sure you fill in the bubble completely with a pencil. The answers to all the exercises in this lesson begin on page 236.

1. Ⓐ Ⓑ Ⓒ Ⓓ   4. Ⓐ Ⓑ Ⓒ Ⓓ
2. Ⓐ Ⓑ Ⓒ Ⓓ   5. Ⓐ Ⓑ Ⓒ Ⓓ
3. Ⓐ Ⓑ Ⓒ Ⓓ

1. Who wanted the states to stay together?
   A. the South
   B. the North
   C. the West
   D. the East

2. One reason for the Civil War was
   A. freedom of the seas
   B. taxes
   C. slavery
   D. bad leaders

3. Who fought during the Civil War?
   A. East and West
   B. West and East
   C. West and North
   D. North and South

4. Who wanted to start their own country?
   A. the South
   B. the North
   C. the West
   D. the East

5. Who won the Civil War?
   A. the South
   B. the North
   C. the East
   D. the West

✎ EXERCISES
Fill In the Blanks

1. _____ wanted to start their own country.   The North   The South

2. During the Civil War the _____ fought.   North/South   East/West

3. _____ was one reason for the Civil War.   Slavery   Taxes

4. The North wanted the states to stay _____.   together   apart

5. The _____ won the Civil War.   South   North

Yes or No Questions

Circle **Yes** if the sentence is true. Circle **No** if the sentence is not true.

Yes   No   The East and West fought during the Civil War.
Yes   No   The South wanted to start their own country.
Yes   No   The South won the Civil War.
Yes   No   The North wanted the states to stay together.
Yes   No   The North and South fought during the Civil War.
Yes   No   One reason for the Civil War was slavery.
Yes   No   The North won the Civil War.

✎ DICTATION PRACTICE

Write each sentence twice. Then have your partner read the sentences to you. Write each sentence as you hear it on a different piece of paper.

1. I wear a hat.

2. I wear a yellow hat.

3. I wear hats.

1. _____.

1. _____.

2. _____.

2. _____.

3. _____.

3. _____.

INTERVIEW PRACTICE

Say these practice questions and answers out loud several times.

Question: Have you ever been declared legally **incompetent** or confined as a patient in a **mental institution?**

Answer: No, I am not crazy.

Question: Were you ever in a mental hospital?

Answer: No, I am mentally competent.

Question: Have you ever been confined as a patient in a **mental institution?**

Answer: No, I've never been in a hospital for people whose minds don't work right.

Question: Were you born with or have you acquired any title of **nobility?**

Answer: No, my parents were factory workers.

Question: Are you a king, queen, duke, earl, prince, or do you have any other title of **nobility?**

Answer: No, I don't have any special titles along with my name and I am not a king or any other noble.

Question: Were you born with or have you acquired any title of **nobility?**
Answer: No, no one in my family is related to a king or queen.

Question: Have you at any time ever ordered, incited, assisted, or otherwise participated in the **persecution** of any person because of race, religion, national origin, or political opinion?
Answer: No, I have never hurt anyone.

Question: Have you at any time ever ordered or otherwise participated in the **persecution** of any person because of race, religion, national origin, or political opinion?
Answer: No, I don't hurt people because of what they believe or what color they are.

Question: Have you ever participated in the **persecution** of any person because of race, religion, national origin, or political opinion?
Answer: No, I have never persecuted anyone.

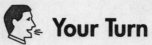 **Your Turn**

Now give your own answers to the interview questions above. Have your partner ask the questions. Then answer them out loud.

LESSON 18

ABRAHAM LINCOLN

Abraham Lincoln

Freed the Slaves

 **QUESTIONS**

Say these questions and answers many times out loud.

1. Who was the President during the Civil War?   Abraham Lincoln

2. What did the Emancipation Proclamation do?   freed many slaves

3. Which President freed the slaves?   Abraham Lincoln

4. What freed the slaves?   Emancipation Proclamation

WORDS TO KNOW

united:	stay together as one
Emancipation Proclamation:	written statement of freedom
noncombatant service:	help the military but not fight
national importance:	helpful to the United States

ABOUT ABRAHAM LINCOLN

Abraham Lincoln was President during the Civil War. He wanted the country to be **united,** and he was against slavery. President Lincoln freed the slaves by writing the **Emancipation Proclamation**. After the war, the **Emancipation Proclamation** became the 13th amendment to the Constitution.

Abraham Lincoln

✏ TEST QUESTIONS

Mark your answers to these test questions in the bubble answer sheet below. Make sure you fill in the bubble completely with a pencil. The answers to all the exercises in this lesson begin on page 237.

1. Ⓐ Ⓑ Ⓒ Ⓓ   3. Ⓐ Ⓑ Ⓒ Ⓓ
2. Ⓐ Ⓑ Ⓒ Ⓓ   4. Ⓐ Ⓑ Ⓒ Ⓓ

1. Who freed the slaves?
   A. President Lincoln
   B. Senator Brown
   C. President Jefferson
   D. President Washington

2. Who was President during the Civil War?
   A. Abraham Lincoln
   B. George Washington
   C. Bill Clinton
   D. Thomas Jefferson

3. What did the Emancipation Proclamation do?
   A. freed the slaves
   B. freed the women
   C. purchased land
   D. expanded the country

4. The slaves were freed by
   A. the Bill of Rights
   B. the Emancipation Proclamation
   C. the Constitution
   D. the Declaration of Independence

✎ EXERCISES
Fill In the Blanks

1. President _____ freed the slaves.   Washington   Lincoln

2. Abraham _____ was President during the Civil War.   Jefferson   Lincoln

3. The Emancipation Proclamation freed the _____.   slaves   colonists

4. The _____ won the Civil War.   South   North

Yes or No Questions

Circle **Yes** if the sentence is true. Circle **No** if the sentence is not true.

Yes   No   George Washington was President during the Civil War.

Yes   No   President Lincoln freed the slaves.

Yes   No   The Emancipation Proclamation freed the slaves.

Yes   No   Abraham Lincoln was President during the Civil War.

Yes   No   The slaves were freed by the Emancipation Proclamation.

Yes   No   The North won the Civil War.

✎ DICTATION PRACTICE

Read each sentence once, try to remember it, and then write it twice.

1. I am learning English.

2. They are learning English.

3. My sisters are learning English.

1. _____.

1. _____.

2. _____.

2. _____.

3. _____.

3. _____.

🗣 INTERVIEW PRACTICE

Say these practice questions and answers out loud several times.

Question: If the law requires it, are you willing to perform **noncombatant services** in the Armed Forces of the United States?

Answer: Yes, I will help the soldiers when the law tells me.

Question: If required by law, are you willing to perform **noncombatant services** in the Armed Forces of the United States?

Answer: Yes, I will do whatever I can to help the military.

Question: Are you willing to perform **noncombatant services** in the Armed Forces of the United States, if the law says you must?

Answer: Yes, I will help the Armed Forces if the law tells me.

Question: If the law requires it, are you willing to perform work of **national importance** under civilian direction?

Answer: Yes, I will do anything to help the United States when the law says I must.

Question: Are you willing to perform work of **national importance** under civilian direction, if required by the law?

Answer: Yes, if the law tells me, I will work to help the United States.

Question: Will you perform work of **national importance** under civilian direction, when the law says you must?

Answer: Yes, I will do anything to help the United States whenever it is needed.

Your Turn

Now give your own answers to the interview questions above. Have your partner ask the questions. Then answer them out loud.

LESSON 19

Later History

1940s, 1950s, 1960s		
World War II	Alaska & Hawaii	Martin Luther King, Jr.

QUESTIONS

Say these questions and answers many times out loud.

1. Who were America's enemies in World War II?

Germany, Italy, and Japan

2. Who were America's allies during World War II?

Britain, Canada, Australia, New Zealand, Russia, China, and France

3. Name one purpose of the United Nations.

for countries to talk about world problems and try to solve them

4. What was the 49th state to join the union?

Alaska

5. What was the 50th state to join the union?

Hawaii

6. Who was Martin Luther King, Jr.?

a civil rights leader

WORDS TO KNOW

enemies: people we fought against
allies: friends during war time
civil rights leader: person who helps others believe in justice for all races of people
drafted: asked to be a soldier

SOME EVENTS IN LATER HISTORY

Another war was going on in the 1940s, called World War II. America's **enemies** in World War II were Germany, Italy, and Japan. America's **allies** during World War II were England, France, China, the Soviet Union, Canada, Australia, and New Zealand. After World War II, the United Nations was created. At the United Nations, many countries talk about world problems and try to solve them in a peaceful way. In the 1950s, Alaska was the 49th state to join the union and Hawaii was the 50th state to join the union. They were the last two states to join the union. During the 1960s, Dr. Martin Luther King, Jr. worked as a **civil rights leader.** He worked for equal rights for black people and others. He led many peaceful demonstrations.

Rev. Dr. Martin Luther King, Jr.

✎ TEST QUESTIONS

Mark your answers to these test questions in the bubble answer sheet below. Make sure you fill in the bubble completely with a pencil. The answers to all the exercises in this lesson begin on page 238.

1. Ⓐ Ⓑ Ⓒ Ⓓ   4. Ⓐ Ⓑ Ⓒ Ⓓ   7. Ⓐ Ⓑ Ⓒ Ⓓ
2. Ⓐ Ⓑ Ⓒ Ⓓ   5. Ⓐ Ⓑ Ⓒ Ⓓ
3. Ⓐ Ⓑ Ⓒ Ⓓ   6. Ⓐ Ⓑ Ⓒ Ⓓ

1. What is one purpose of the United Nations?
   A. to raise taxes
   B. for countries to talk about world problems and try to solve them
   C. to declare wars
   D. to make and enforce laws

2. What was the 49th state to join the union?
   A. Minnesota
   B. New York
   C. Texas
   D. Alaska

3. Who were America's enemies in World War II?
   A. Germany, Italy, and Japan
   B. Canada, Russia, and Poland
   C. Mexico and Brazil
   D. Britain and France

4. What was the 50th state to join the union?
   A. New Jersey
   B. Rhode Island
   C. Hawaii
   D. Wisconsin

5. Who was Martin Luther King, Jr.?
   A. civil rights leader
   B. President
   C. senator
   D. tax collector

6. Who were America's allies during World War II?
   A. Mexico and Brazil
   B. Chile, Argentina, and Venezuela
   C. Britain, Canada, Australia, New Zealand, Russia, China, and France
   D. Syria, Egypt, Iraq, and Africa

7. The last states to be added to the United States were
   A. Alaska and Hawaii
   B. Puerto Rico and Hawaii
   C. Guam and Hawaii
   D. Alaska and Puerto Rico

✏ EXERCISES
Circle the Correct Answer

1.	Who were two of America's enemies in World War II?	Britain/Canada	Japan/Italy
2.	Who were two of America's allies in World War II?	Britain/Canada	Japan/Italy
3.	Where do countries talk about world problems and try to solve them?	United Nations	United Justices
4.	What was the 49th state to join the union?	Alaska	Connecticut
5.	What was the 50th state to join the union?	Utah	Hawaii
6.	Who was a civil rights leader?	Martin Luther King, Jr.	Francis Scott Key

Yes or No Questions

Circle **Yes** if the sentence is true. Circle **No** if the sentence is not true.

Yes	No	Germany and Japan were two of America's enemies in World War II.
Yes	No	China and Britain were two of America's allies in World War II.
Yes	No	Countries talk about world problems and try to solve them at the United Nations.
Yes	No	Wyoming was the 49th state to join the union.

Yes   No   Hawaii was the 50th state to join the union.
Yes   No   Martin Luther King, Jr. was a civil rights leader.
Yes   No   Russia and France were two of America's allies in World War II.
Yes   No   Martin Luther King, Jr. was a congressman.

✏ DICTATION PRACTICE

Write each sentence twice. For the first time, copy the sentence. For the second time, have your partner read the sentence while you write it.

1. I like snow.
2. Today it is snowing.
3. The snow is cold.

1. _____.

1. _____.

2. _____.

2. _____.

3. _____.

3. _____.

INTERVIEW PRACTICE

Say these practice questions and answers out loud several times.

Question: Have you ever left the United States to avoid being **drafted** into the U.S. Armed Forces?

Answer: No, I have never gone away to avoid going into the military.

Question: Have you ever left the United States to avoid being **drafted?**

Answer: No, I have never left the country so I didn't have to go to war.

Question: Have you ever left the United States so you didn't have to fight in a war?

Answer: No, I have never gone away to avoid being **drafted** into the military.

Question: Have you ever failed to comply with Selective Service laws?

Answer: No, I never withheld my name for becoming a soldier.

Question: Have you ever failed to comply with Selective Service laws?

Answer: No, I have always given my name so I could be called to fight.

Question: Did you register for the Selective Service?

Answer: Yes, I gave my name to the government.

Question: Do you know your Selective Service number?

Answer: Yes, I have that number written on this paper.

Your Turn

Now give your own answers to the interview questions above. Have your partner ask the questions. Then answer them out loud.

LESSON 20

The United States Today

Politics Today

| Democrats & Republicans | Democratic Republic | Our Democracy |

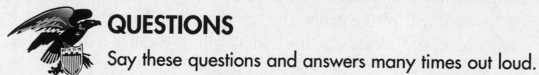

QUESTIONS

Say these questions and answers many times out loud.

1. How many states are in the United States?   fifty (50)

2. Where is the capital of the U.S.?   Washington, DC

3. What are the two major political parties in the U.S.?   Democrat and Republican

4. What kind of government does the U.S. have?   Democratic Republic

WORDS TO KNOW

political party:	group with similar ideas about government
Democratic Republic:	the form of the U.S. government
democracy:	government of, by, and for the people
exemption:	to stay out of
deserted:	left the military without permission
alienage:	status of being a foreign-born resident
conscientious objections:	reasons a person will not fight in a war

ABOUT THE UNITED STATES TODAY

In the United States today, there are fifty states. The capital of the United States is in Washington, DC. The two major **political parties** in the U.S. are the Democrats and Republicans. The government of the U.S. is a **Democratic Republic,** which Abraham Lincoln called a "government of the people, by the people, and for the people." A government where the people decide who the leaders will be is called a **democracy.**

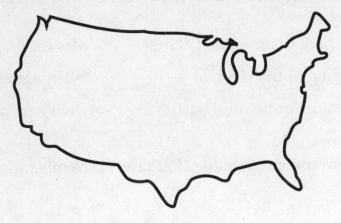

The United States

✎ TEST QUESTIONS

Mark your answers to these test questions in the bubble answer sheet below. Make sure you fill in the bubble completely with a pencil. The answers to all the exercises in this lesson begin on page 239.

1. Ⓐ Ⓑ Ⓒ Ⓓ   3. Ⓐ Ⓑ Ⓒ Ⓓ
2. Ⓐ Ⓑ Ⓒ Ⓓ   4. Ⓐ Ⓑ Ⓒ Ⓓ

1. Where is the capital of the United States?
   A. New York City
   B. Washington, DC
   C. Philadelphia, PA
   D. Los Angeles

2. What kind of government does the U.S. have?
   A. Democratic Republic
   B. Feudalism
   C. Communist
   D. Republic of States

3. How many states are in the union?
   A. forty-four
   B. forty-eight
   C. fifty
   D. fifty-two

4. What are the two major political parties in the U.S.?
   A. Democrat and Republican
   B. Communist and Fascist
   C. Judicial and Republican
   D. Executive and Democratic

✏ EXERCISES
Fill In the Blanks

1. Democrat and Republican are the two major _____ in the United States.

   political parties   companies

2. There are _____ states in America.

   fifty   thirteen

3. _____ and Republican are the two major political parties in the United States.

   Congress   Democrat

4. The United States has a Democratic _____ form of government.

   Republic   States

5. The capital of the United States is in _____.

   New York City   Washington, DC

Yes or No Questions

Circle **Yes** if the sentence is true. Circle **No** if the sentence is not true.

Yes   No   The capital of the United States is in New York City.

Yes   No   The United States has a Democratic Republic form of government.

Yes   No   There are fifty states in America.

Yes   No   Democrat and Republican are the two major political parties in the United States.

Yes   No   The United States has a Communist form of government.

Yes   No   The capital of the United States is in Washington, DC.

Yes   No   The United States is made up of fifty states.

✏ DICTATION PRACTICE

Write each sentence twice. For the first time, copy the sentence. For the second time, try to write the sentence from memory.

1. The child plays.

2. The child plays with a toy.

3. The child likes the toy.

1. _____.

1. _____.

2. _____.

2. _____.

3. _____.

3. _____.

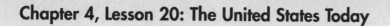 ## INTERVIEW PRACTICE

Say these practice questions and answers out loud several times.

Question: Did you ever apply for **exemption** from military service because of **alienage, conscientious objections,** or other reasons?

Answer: No, I have never said that I would not fight for America.

Question: Have you ever tried to avoid military service?

Answer: No, I have always been willing to be a soldier.

Question: Did you ever request to stay out of the Armed Forces because of your religious beliefs?

Answer: No, my religion says it is okay to protect my country by fighting a war.

Question: Have you ever **deserted** from the military, air, or naval forces of the United States?

Answer: No, I have never even been in the Armed Forces.

Question:	Have you ever **deserted** from the military, air, or naval forces of the United States?
Answer:	No, I was honorably discharged from the army.

Question:	Did you leave the Armed Forces before you were allowed to?
Answer:	No, I was in the Armed Forces for a full three years.

Your Turn

Now give your own answers to the interview questions above. Have your partner ask the questions. Then answer them out loud.

LESSON 21

The Flag

The Flag	
50 Stars	13 Stripes

 ## QUESTIONS

Say these questions and answers many times out loud.

1. What are the colors of our flag? — red, white, blue

2. How many stars are on our flag? — fifty (50)

3. What color are the stars on our flag? — white

4. What do the stars on the flag represent? — The fifty (50) states. There is one star for each state in the union.

5. How many stripes are on the flag? — thirteen (13)

6. What color are the stripes? — red and white

7. What do the stripes on the flag represent? — original thirteen (13) colonies

8. Who wrote "The Star-Spangled Banner"? — Francis Scott Key

9. What is the national anthem of the United States? — "The Star-Spangled Banner"

WORDS TO KNOW

represent:	stand for
national anthem:	song about America
banner:	flag
Communist:	person who belongs to a party that wants common ownership of production and distribution of products

ABOUT THE FLAG

The United States has a flag that is red, white, and blue. There are fifty white stars that **represent** the fifty states in the union. There are thirteen red and white stripes that **represent** the original thirteen colonies. Our **national anthem** is about the flag. The name of our **national anthem** is "The Star-Spangled **Banner**," and it was written by Francis Scott Key.

The American Flag

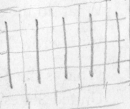

✏ TEST QUESTIONS

Mark your answers to these test questions in the bubble answer sheet below. Make sure you fill in the bubble completely with a pencil. The answers to all the exercises in this lesson begin on page 240.

1. Ⓐ Ⓑ Ⓒ Ⓓ   4. Ⓐ Ⓑ Ⓒ Ⓓ   7. Ⓐ Ⓑ Ⓒ Ⓓ
2. Ⓐ Ⓑ Ⓒ Ⓓ   5. Ⓐ Ⓑ Ⓒ Ⓓ   8. Ⓐ Ⓑ Ⓒ Ⓓ
3. Ⓐ Ⓑ Ⓒ Ⓓ   6. Ⓐ Ⓑ Ⓒ Ⓓ   9. Ⓐ Ⓑ Ⓒ Ⓓ

1. How many stars are on the flag?
   A. thirteen
   B. forty-four
   C. fifty
   D. fifty-two

2. What are the colors of our flag?
   A. red, white, blue
   B. blue, orange, red
   C. red, white, pink
   D. red, white, green

3. How many stripes are on the flag?
   A. ten
   B. thirteen
   C. fifty
   D. fifty-two

4. What color are the stars on the flag?
   A. red
   B. white
   C. blue
   D. black

5. What do the stripes on the flag represent?
   A. fifty states
   B. original thirteen colonies
   C. Mayflower
   D. pilgrims

6. What do the stars on the flag represent?
   A. fifty states
   B. original thirteen colonies
   C. Mayflower
   D. pilgrims

7. What colors are the stripes?
   A. red and white
   B. blue and white
   C. white and blue
   D. red and blue

8. What is the national anthem of the United States?
   A. The Star-Spangled Banner
   B. My Country
   C. America the Beautiful
   D. Good News America

9. Who wrote "The Star-Spangled Banner"?
   A. Abraham Lincoln
   B. Senator Brown
   C. Francis Scott Key
   D. George Washington

✏ EXERCISES
Matching Questions

Match the correct answer to each question.

_____What do the stripes on the flag represent?   A. red, white, blue
_____What color are the stripes?   B. fifty
_____Who wrote "The Star-Spangled Banner"?   C. white
_____What color are the stars on the flag?   D. fifty states
_____How many stripes are on the flag?   E. thirteen
_____What do the stars on the flag represent?   F. Francis Scott Key
_____What are the colors of our flag?   G. red and white

_____How many stars are on the flag?   H. original thirteen colonies

_____What is the national anthem of the   I. "The Star-Spangled Banner"
            United States?

Yes or No Questions

Circle **Yes** if the sentence is true. Circle **No** if the sentence is not true.

Yes	No	The stars on the flag are white.
Yes	No	The flag is red, white, and blue.
Yes	No	The stripes on the flag represent the original thirteen colonies.
Yes	No	The flag has twelve stripes on it.
Yes	No	Francis Scott Key wrote "The Star-Spangled Banner."
Yes	No	The stripes on the flag are red and white.
Yes	No	The stars on the flag represent the fifty stars in the sky.
Yes	No	The stars on the flag are blue.
Yes	No	"The Star-Spangled Banner" is the national anthem of the United States.
Yes	No	The flag has fifty stars on it.

✎ DICTATION PRACTICE

Write each sentence twice. Then have your partner read the sentences to you. Write each sentence as you hear it on a different piece of paper.

1. I can read English.

2. I can write English.

3. I can read, write, and speak English.

1. _____.

1. _____.

2. _____.

2. _____.

3. _____.

3. _____.

🗣️ INTERVIEW PRACTICE

Say these practice questions and answers out loud several times.

Question: Are you a member of the **Communist** Party?
Answer: No, I am not a member of any group.

Question: Have you ever been a member of the **Communist** Party?
Answer: No, I never joined that group.

Question: Are you now or have you ever been a member of the **Communist** Party?
Answer: I am not a member now, but I was many years ago.

Question: Why were you a **Communist?**
Answer: I joined because everyone else joined. I didn't believe in it.

Question: When was that?
Answer: I joined in 1972, but I never went to the meetings.

🗣️ Your Turn

Now give your own answers to the interview questions above. Have your partner ask the questions. Then answer them out loud.

LESSON 22

State and Local Governments

State & Local Governments

State Capital   Governor   Two Senators

Mayor

QUESTIONS

Write in the answers to these questions and then say the questions and answers many times out loud.

1. What is the capital of your state? _____

2. Who is the current governor of your state? _____ Brad Henry

3. Who are the two senators from your state? _____

4. Who is the head of your local government? _____ Humphrey

WORDS TO KNOW

capital: city where the government is located

affiliated: linked or connected

ABOUT STATE AND LOCAL GOVERNMENTS

Each state has its own **capital**. You need to know what the **capital** of your state is. For example, the **capital** of Texas is Austin, the **capital** of New York state is Albany, and the **capital** of Florida is Tallahassee. Every state has a governor as its head executive. Find out who the governor is in your state. Each state also has two senators who represent that state in Washington, DC. Who are the two senators from your state? Within each state are many local governments. Who is the head of your local government? Find out the name of your mayor.

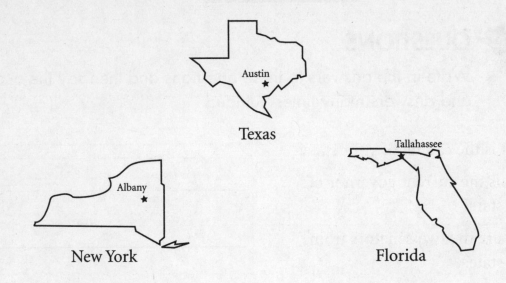

✏ EXERCISES
Fill In the Blanks

1. The head of your local government is _____.

2. _____ is the capital of your state.

3. The governor of your state is _____.

4. The two senators from your state are _____ and _____.

5. _____ is the mayor of your city.

Copy the Sentences

Copy each sentence below two times after you fill in the blank.

1. The head of my local government is _____.

    _____.

    _____.

2. The governor of my state is _____.

    _____.

    _____.

3. The two senators from my state are _____ and _____.

    _____.

    _____.

✏ DICTATION PRACTICE

Write each sentence twice. For the first time, copy the sentence. For the second time, have your partner read the sentence while you write it.

1. Today is Tuesday.

2. Tomorrow is Wednesday.

3. Today it is windy.

1. _____ .

1. _____ .

2. _____ .

2. _____ .

3. _____ .

3. _____ .

🗣 INTERVIEW PRACTICE

Say these practice questions and answers out loud several times.

Question: Have you ever been **affiliated** with the Nazi Party?
Answer: No, I don't agree with the Nazi Party.

Question: Have you ever been a member of the Nazi Party?
Answer: No, I never joined the Nazi Party.

Question:	Did you help the Nazi government in any way?
Answer:	No, I never assisted the Nazis.

Question:	Were you a part of the Nazi Party between 1933 and 1945?
Answer:	No, I don't agree with the Nazi Party.

Question:	Have you ever helped the Nazi Party?
Answer:	No, I don't like the Nazi Party.

Question:	Are you a member of any clubs or organizations?
Answer:	No, I am not a part of any organized groups.

Question:	Are you a member of any clubs or organizations?
Answer:	Yes, I am a member of the Small Business Association.

Question:	Are you a member of any clubs?
Answer:	No, I do not take part in any clubs.

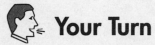 **Your Turn**

Now give your own answers to the interview questions above. Have your partner ask the questions. Then answer them out loud.

LESSON 23

American Citizens

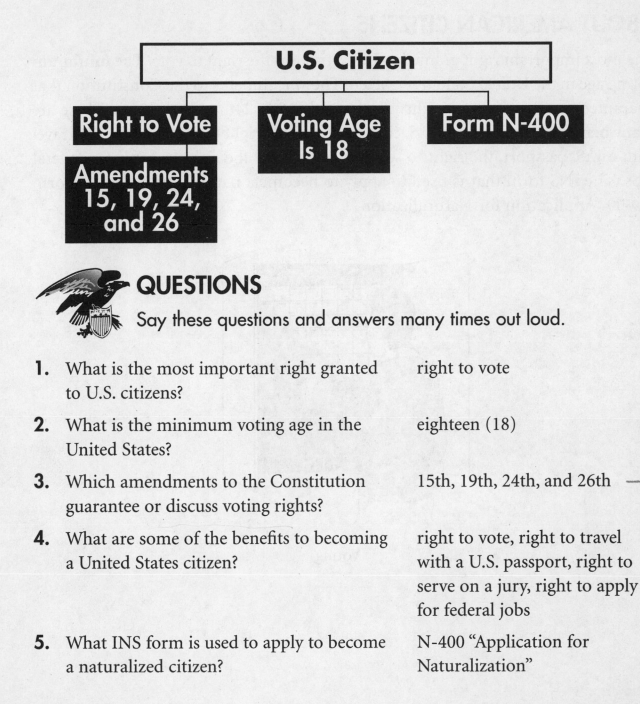

U.S. Citizen		
Right to Vote	**Voting Age Is 18**	**Form N-400**
Amendments 15, 19, 24, and 26		

QUESTIONS

Say these questions and answers many times out loud.

1. What is the most important right granted to U.S. citizens?

right to vote

2. What is the minimum voting age in the United States?

eighteen (18)

3. Which amendments to the Constitution guarantee or discuss voting rights?

15th, 19th, 24th, and 26th

4. What are some of the benefits to becoming a United States citizen?

right to vote, right to travel with a U.S. passport, right to serve on a jury, right to apply for federal jobs

5. What INS form is used to apply to become a naturalized citizen?

N-400 "Application for Naturalization"

WORDS TO KNOW

minimum: the lowest number allowed
benefits: good things
false testimony: tell a lie

ABOUT AMERICAN CITIZENS

The most important right granted to U.S. citizens is the right to vote. The **minimum** voting age in the United States is eighteen. The amendments to the Constitution that guarantee or discuss voting rights are the 15th, 19th, 24th, and the 26th. There are many **benefits** to becoming a U.S. citizen, such as the right to vote, the right to travel with a U.S. passport, the right to serve on a jury, and the right to apply for federal jobs. The INS form that is used to apply to become a naturalized citizen is Form N-400 "Application for Naturalization."

Voting

✏ TEST QUESTIONS

Mark your answers to these test questions in the bubble answer sheet below. Make sure you fill in the bubble completely with a pencil. The answers to all the exercises in this lesson begin on page 241.

1. Ⓐ   Ⓑ   Ⓒ   Ⓓ   4. Ⓐ   Ⓑ   Ⓒ   Ⓓ
2. Ⓐ   Ⓑ   Ⓒ   Ⓓ   5. Ⓐ   Ⓑ   Ⓒ   Ⓓ
3. Ⓐ   Ⓑ   Ⓒ   Ⓓ

1. Which of the following is a benefit of becoming a U.S. citizen?
   A. right to pay taxes
   B. right to vote
   C. right to go to school
   D. right to work

2. Which amendment to the Constitution guarantees or discusses voting rights?
   A. third
   B. fifth
   C. twelfth
   D. fifteenth

3. What is the minimum voting age in the United States?
   A. sixteen
   B. eighteen
   C. twenty-one
   D. twenty-five

4. What is the most important right granted to U.S. citizens?
   A. right to work
   B. right to pay taxes
   C. right to go to school
   D. right to vote

5. What INS form is used to apply to become a naturalized citizen?
   A. N-200 "Petition for Naturalization"
   B. N-400 "Application for Naturalization"
   C. Social Security Card
   D. Form 2000

✎ EXERCISES
Circle the Correct Answer

1. Which amendment to the Constitution guarantees or discusses voting rights?

   third   twenty-forth

2. What is the most important right granted to U.S. citizens?

   right to vote   right to work

3. What is the minimum voting age in the United States?

   sixteen   eighteen

4. What is a benefit of becoming a U.S. citizen?

   right to travel with a U.S. passport   right to own a home

5. What INS form is used to apply to become a naturalized citizen?

   N-400 "Application for Naturalization"   N-200 "Petition for Naturalization"

Yes or No Questions

Circle **Yes** if the sentence is true. Circle **No** if the sentence is not true.

Yes   No   The minimum voting age in the United States is twenty-one.

Yes   No   The right to vote is the most important right granted to U.S. citizens.

Yes   No   The right to travel with a U.S. passport is granted to U.S. citizens.

Yes   No   The 15th, 19th, 24th, and 26th amendments to the Constitution guarantee or discuss voting rights.

Yes   No   The right to bear arms is the most important right granted to U.S. citizens.

Yes   No   The N-400 "Application for Naturalization" is the INS form you use to apply to become a U.S. citizen.

Yes   No   Eighteen is the minimum voting age in the United States.

✏ DICTATION PRACTICE

Read each sentence once, try to remember it, and then write it twice.

1. It is cold.
2. It is cold outside.
3. I like cold weather.

1. _____.

1. _____.

2. _____.

2. _____.

3. _____.

3. _____.

👥 INTERVIEW PRACTICE

Say these practice questions and answers out loud several times.

Question:	Have you ever given **false testimony** to obtain an immigration benefit?
Answer:	No, I have never lied.

Question:	Have you ever lied to obtain an immigration benefit?
Answer:	No, I have never given **false testimony**.

Question: Have you ever lied at an immigration interview when you were under oath?

Answer: No, I have never lied after swearing to tell the truth.

Question: If the law requires it, are you willing to bear arms on behalf of the United States?

Answer: Yes, I will fight in a war to help the United States.

Question: If the law requires it, are you willing to bear arms on behalf of the United States?

Answer: Yes, I will be a soldier if the law tells me.

Question: Are you willing to bear arms for the United States, even if it is against the country you used to live in?

Answer: Yes, I will fight for America even if it is against my old country.

Your Turn

Now give your own answers to the interview questions above. Have your partner ask the questions. Then answer them out loud.

REVIEW TEST 6

Mark your answers to these test questions in the bubble answer sheet on page 40. Make sure you fill in the bubble completely with a pencil. The answers to this test are given on page 242.

1. How many senators does your state have?
   A. one
   B. two
   C. three
   D. four

2. Which countries were our enemies during World War II?
   A. Mexico, Canada, England
   B. Spain, Italy, France
   C. Russia, France, England
   D. Germany, Italy, Japan

3. Who was Martin Luther King, Jr.?
   A. President
   B. Supreme Court justice
   C. civil rights leader
   D. governor

4. What are the 49th and 50th states of the union?
   A. Iowa and Minnesota
   B. Michigan and Illinois
   C. Washington and Montana
   D. Alaska and Hawaii

5. What is the minimum voting age in the United States?
   A. seventeen
   B. sixteen
   C. twenty-one
   D. eighteen

6. What is the most important right granted to U.S. citizens?
   A. right to vote
   B. right to bear arms
   C. right to travel
   D. right to work

7. How many states are in the union?
   A. thirty
   B. forty
   C. fifty
   D. sixty

8. What are the two main political parties in the U.S.?
   A. Communist and Fascist
   B. Democrat and Republican
   C. Partisan and Democratic
   D. Judicial and Republican

9. What form of government does the U.S. have?
   A. Democratic Republic
   B. Communist
   C. Fascist
   D. Fundamentalist

10. What are the colors of our flag?
   A. red, white, blue
   B. blue, orange, red
   C. red, white, pink
   D. red, white, green

11. How many stripes are on the flag?
   A. ten
   B. thirteen
   C. fifty
   D. fifty-two

12. What do the stripes on the flag represent?
   A. fifty states
   B. original thirteen colonies
   C. Mayflower
   D. pilgrims

13. What do the stars on the flag represent?
   A. fifty states
   B. original thirteen colonies
   C. Mayflower
   D. pilgrims

14. Who were America's allies during World War II?
   A. Mexico and Brazil
   B. Chile, Argentina, and Venezuela
   C. Britain, Canada, Australia, New Zealand, Russia, China, and France
   D. Syria, Egypt, Iraq, and Africa

15. What is one purpose of the United Nations?
   A. to raise taxes
   B. for countries to talk about world problems and try to solve them
   C. to declare wars
   D. to make and enforce laws

CHAPTER 5

Words to Know

Here is a list of all the vocabulary from the twenty-three lessons in Chapter 4. Study this list to learn what each word means. This list will help you to pass your citizenship exam. Each word is also given in Spanish to help Spanish-speaking readers.

WORD A	SPANISH	WHAT IT MEANS
address	dirección	where you live
adopted	adoptado	put into effect
advises	aconsejar	gives help to
affiliated	afiliado	linked or connected
alienage	extranjería	status of being a foreign-born resident
allies	aliados	friends during war time
amendments	enmiendas	changes
appointed	nombrado	chosen or selected
arrested	arrestado	formally charged by a police officer

WORD	SPANISH	WHAT IT MEANS
B		
banner	bandera	flag
basic belief	creencia fundamental	main idea, most important part
bear arms	portar armas	carry a gun
benefits	beneficios	good things
Bill of Rights	la Declaración de Derechos	first ten amendments
birth place	lugar de nacimiento	country where you were born
born	nacer	when a baby comes into the world
branches	divisiones	separate parts

C		
Cabinet	Gabinete	fourteen people who help the President make decisions
capital	capital	city where the government is located
Capitol	Capitolio	where Congress meets
chief justice	juez principal	head of the Supreme Court
citizenship	ciudadanía	the country where you have the right to fully participate in the benefits and laws of that country
civil rights leader	líder de derechos civiles	person who helps others believe in justice for all races of people
Civil War	la Guerra de Secesión	war between the North and South
claimed	pretendido	said something was true; pretended
colonies	colonias	original thirteen states in America
Communist	Comunista	person who belongs to a party that wants common ownership of production and distribution of products

WORD	SPANISH	WHAT IT MEANS
Congress	el Congreso	people who make our laws
conscientious objections	objeción de conciencia	reasons a person will not fight in a war
Constitution	la Constitución	supreme law of the United States
crime	delito	breaking the law

D

Declaration of Independence	la Declaración de la Independencia	written statement saying the colonies wanted to be free from England
democracy	democracia	government of, by, and for the people
Democratic Republic	República Democrática	the form of the U.S. government
deported	deportado	a judge in court ordered you to go back to your first country
deserted	desertado	left the military without permission
different	distinto	another
drafted	llamado a filas	asked to be a soldier

E

Electoral College	Colegio Electoral	group who elects the President
Emancipation Proclamation	la Proclamación de la Emancipación de los esclavos	written statement of freedom
employer	patrón	the name of the company or person you work for
enemies	enemigos	people we fight in a war

WORD	SPANISH	WHAT IT MEANS
executive branch	poder ejecutivo	the part of the government made up of the President, Vice President, and Cabinet
exemption	exención	to stay out of

F, G, H

WORD	SPANISH	WHAT IT MEANS
false testimony	testimonio falso	tell a lie
governor	gobernador	leader of a state
habitual drunkard	borracho	person who drinks too much alcohol
head executive	director ejecutivo	the leader or person in charge

I

WORD	SPANISH	WHAT IT MEANS
illegal drugs	drogas ilegales	narcotics, cocaine, marijuana, dope, speed
illegal gambling	juego ilegal	to play cards for money at someone's house
inaugurated	investido	sworn into office
income tax	impuesto sobre la renta	if you work in America, this is the money you pay to the government
incompetent	incompetente	mind does not work (crazy)
independence	independencia	freedom
Independence Day	el Día de la Independencia	July 4th
interpret	interpretar	to explain
introduction	introducción	the beginning

WORD J, L	SPANISH	WHAT IT MEANS
job	deber	work or duty
judicial branch	poder judicial	the part of the government that includes the Supreme Court
legislative branch	poder legislativo	Congress
liberty	libertad	freedom

M

maiden name	apellido de soltera	a woman's last name before getting married
marital status	estado civil	if you are single, married, or divorced
mayor	alcalde	leader of a city
mental institution	manicomio	hospital for people whose minds don't work
minimum	mínimo	the lowest number allowed

N

national anthem	himno nacional	song about America
national importance	interés nacional	helpful to the United States
Native Americans	Indio Americano	people who lived in America when the pilgrims arrived
natural born citizen	ciudadano de nacimiento	person who is born in a country
nobility	nobleza	family is king or queen or is related to them
noncombatant service	servicio de no combate	help the military but not fight

WORD	SPANISH	WHAT IT MEANS
O		
oath	juramento	promise to tell the truth
Oath of Allegiance	Juramento de Lealtad	officially swear to help the United States
occupation	ocupación	the name of your job
P		
persecution	persecución	hurt someone because of their race, religion, national origin, or political opinion
pilgrims	peregrinos	people who came to America on a ship called the Mayflower
political party	partido político	group with similar ideas about government
polygamy	poligamia	having more than one husband or one wife at the same time
port of entry	puerto de entrada	place where you arrived in the country
preamble	preámbulo	the introduction to the Constitution
prostitute	prostituta	to sell your body for money
R		
re-elected	reelegido	voted into office again
registered	inscrito	officially signed up to do something
represent	representar	stand for
representatives	representantes	people who work in the House of Representatives
Revolutionary War	la Guerra de la Independencia	war between the thirteen colonies and England

WORDS	SPANISH	WHAT IT MEANS
senators	senadores	people who work in the Senate
slave	esclavo	someone who is owned by another person
smuggle	pasar de contrabando	illegally sneaking someone or something into the country
Supreme Court	el Tribunal Supremo	highest court in the United States

T

term	período	how long someone works in government
tried	juzgado	put through a trial with a judge and jury

U, W

union	unión	United States of America
united	unido	stay together as one
warrant	orden judicial	official permission from a judge
White House	Casa Blanca	place where President lives while serving as President

CHAPTER 6

Official INS History and Civics Questions

Here is a list, arranged by category, of all the official INS history and civics questions and answers. You need to know the answers to many of these questions. Cover the answers and try to answer each question correctly. Then look at the answers to see if you are correct. All of these questions have already appeared in the twenty-three lessons in Chapter 4.

☆ THE GOVERNMENT STRUCTURE

1. How many branches are there in the government?

   1. three (3)

2. What are the three branches of our government?

   2. executive, legislative, judicial

☆ LEGISLATIVE BRANCH

3. What is the legislative branch of our government?

   3. Congress

4. Who makes the laws in the United States?

   4. Congress

5. What is Congress?

   5. Senate and House of Representatives

6. What are the duties of Congress?

7. Who elects Congress?

8. Where does Congress meet?

9. How many senators are there in Congress?

10. Why are there 100 senators in Congress?

11. Who are the two senators from your state?

12. How long do we elect each senator?

13. How many times can a senator be re-elected?

14. How many representatives are there in Congress?

15. How long do we elect the representatives?

16. How many times can a representative be re-elected?

☆ JUDICIAL BRANCH

17. What is the judicial branch of our government?

18. What are the duties of the Supreme Court?

19. Who is the chief justice of the Supreme Court?

20. Who selects the Supreme Court justices?

21. How many Supreme Court justices are there?

22. What is the highest court in the United States?

6. to make laws

7. the people

8. Capitol in Washington, DC

9. 100 (one hundred)

10. two (2) from each state

11. Ask someone for the answer.

12. six (6) years

13. no limit

14. 435 (four hundred thirty-five)

15. two (2) years

16. no limit

17. Supreme Court

18. to interpret laws

19. William Rehnquist

20. President

21. nine (9)

22. Supreme Court

☆ EXECUTIVE BRANCH

23. What is the executive branch of our government?

23. President, Vice President, Cabinet

24. Who was the first President of the United States?

24. George Washington

25. Who is the President of the United States today?

25. Bill Clinton

26. Who is the Vice President today?

26. Al Gore

27. Who elects the President of the United States?

27. the Electoral College

28. How long do we elect the President?

28. four (4) years

29. Who becomes President of the United States if the President should die?

29. Vice President

30. How many terms can a President serve?

30. two (2)

31. Who becomes President of the United States if the President and Vice President should die?

31. Speaker of the House of Representatives

32. What are the requirements to be President?

32. natural born citizen of the U.S., thirty-five (35) years old, lived in the U.S. fourteen (14) years

33. What special group advises the President?

33. Cabinet

34. What is the White House?

34. President's official home

35. Where is the White House located?

35. Washington, DC

36. In what month do we vote for the President?

36. November

37. In what month is the new President inaugurated?

37. January

38. What is the head executive of a state government called?

38. governor

39. What is the head executive of a city government called?

39. mayor

40. Who signs bills into law?

40. President

41. What is the name of the President's official home?

41. White House

42. Who is commander in chief of the U.S. military?

42. President

43. Who has the power to declare war?

43. Congress

★ THE CONSTITUTION

44. What is the Constitution?

44. the supreme law of the land

45. Can the Constitution be changed?

45. yes

46. What do we call changes to the Constitution?

46. amendments

47. How many amendments are there?

47. twenty-seven (27)

48. What is the supreme law of the United States?

48. Constitution

49. When was the Constitution written?

49. 1787

50. What is the Bill of Rights?

50. the first ten (10) amendments

51. Where does freedom of speech come from?

51. the Bill of Rights

52. Whose rights are guaranteed by the Constitution and the Bill of Rights?

52. everyone in America, including non-citizens

53. What is the introduction to the Constitution called?

53. the preamble

54. What are the first ten amendments to the Constitution called?

55. Name three rights or freedoms guaranteed by the Bill of Rights.

54. the Bill of Rights

55.
1. The freedom of speech, press, and religion
2. Right to bear arms
3. Government may not put soldiers in people's homes
4. Government may not search or take a person's property without a warrant
5. A person may not be tried for the same crime twice
6. A person charged with a crime has rights including the right to a trial and a lawyer
7. People are protected from unreasonable fines or cruel punishment

56. Name one right guaranteed by the first amendment.

56. freedom of: speech, press, religion, peaceable assembly, and requesting change of government

57. What is the most important right granted to U.S. citizens?

57. right to vote

58. What is the minimum voting age in the United States?

58. eighteen (18)

☆ UNITED STATES HISTORY

59. What is the 4th of July?

59. Independence Day

60. When was the Declaration of Independence adopted?

60. July 4, 1776

61. What is the basic belief of the Declaration of Independence?

61. All men are created equal.

62. Who was the main writer of the Declaration of Independence?

62. Thomas Jefferson

63. What is the date of Independence Day?

63. July 4th

64. Which President was the first commander in chief of the U.S. military?

64. George Washington

65. Who did the United States gain independence from?

65. England

66. What country did we fight during the Revolutionary War?

66. England

67. Who said, "Give me liberty or give me death"?

67. Patrick Henry

68. Which President is called the "father of our country"?

68. George Washington

69. Why did the pilgrims come to America?

69. religious freedom

70. Who helped the pilgrims in America?

70. Native Americans

71. What ship brought the pilgrims to America?

71. Mayflower

72. What holiday was celebrated for the first time by the American colonists?

72. Thanksgiving

73. What were the thirteen original states called?

73. colonies

74. Can you name the original thirteen states?

74. Connecticut, New Hampshire, New York, New Jersey, Massachusetts, Pennsylvania, Delaware, Virginia, North Carolina, South Carolina, Georgia, Rhode Island, Maryland

75. Who wrote "The Star-Spangled Banner"?

75. Francis Scott Key

76. What is the national anthem of the United States?

76. "The Star-Spangled Banner"

77. Who was the President during the Civil War?

77. Abraham Lincoln

78. What did the Emancipation Proclamation do?

78. freed many slaves

79. Which President freed the slaves?

79. Abraham Lincoln

80. What are the 49th and 50th states of the union?

80. Alaska and Hawaii

81. Who were America's enemies in World War II?

81. Germany, Italy, and Japan

82. Who was Martin Luther King, Jr.?

82. a civil rights leader

☆ THE FLAG

83. What are the colors of our flag?

83. red, white, blue

84. How many stars are on our flag?

84. fifty (50)

85. What color are the stars on our flag?

85. white

86. What do the stars on the flag represent?

86. The fifty (50) states. There is one star for each state in the union.

87. How many stripes are on the flag?

87. thirteen (13)

88. What color are the stripes?

88. red and white

89. What do the stripes on the flag represent?

89. original thirteen (13) colonies

☆ YOUR STATE GOVERNMENT

90. What is the capital of your state?

90. Each state has a different answer. Find out what the capital of your state is.

91. Who is the current governor of your state?

91. Each state has a different answer. Find out who the governor of your state is.

92. Who is the head of your local government?

92. Find out the name of your mayor.

☆ THE UNITED STATES TODAY

93. How many states are there in the United States?

93. fifty (50)

94. Name one purpose of the United Nations.

94. for countries to talk about world problems and try to solve them

95. Name one benefit of becoming a citizen of the United States.

95. right to vote, right to travel with a U.S. passport, right to serve on a jury, right to apply for federal jobs

96. What are the two major political parties in the U.S. today?

96. Democrat and Republican

97. What kind of government does the U.S. have?

97. Democratic Republic

98. What is the United States Capitol?

98. place where Congress meets

99. Where is the capital of the United States?

99. Washington, D.C.

100. What INS form is used to apply to become a naturalized citizen?

100. Form N-400 "Application for Naturalization"

CHAPTER 7

Typical N-400 Questions and Answers

Here are many questions, with sample answers, that you may be asked during your INS interview or on the N-400 application form when you apply for naturalization. Most of these questions have already appeared in the lessons in Chapter 4. The highlighted words are ones you'll find definitions for in Chapter 5. Practice answering the questions using your own information. Have a partner read the questions out loud to you and then answer them.

Question: Do you understand what an **oath** is?
Answer: Yes, it is a promise to tell the truth.

Question: What is your complete name?
Answer: My name is Yolanda Rodriguez Martinez.

Question: What is your name?
Answer: Yolanda Rodriguez Martinez.

Question: What is your **address?**
Answer: My address is 423 Tenth Avenue, Brooklyn, New York 11209.

Question: Where do you live?
Answer: I live at 423 Tenth Avenue, Brooklyn, New York 11209.

Question: What is your home phone number?
Answer: My home phone number is 718-555-7889.

Question: What is your telephone number at home?
Answer: It is 718-555-7889.

Question: Do you have a work telephone number?
Answer: Yes, my work number is 212-555-6000.

Question: What is your work phone number?
Answer: My work phone number is 212-555-6000.

Question: Do you have a work number?
Answer: No, I am not currently working.

Question: May I see your passport?
Answer: Yes, here it is.

Question: Do you have your passport with you?
Answer: Yes, I do.

Question: What is your current **citizenship**?
Answer: I am currently a citizen of Mexico.

Question: Your current **citizenship** is?
Answer: Mexican.

Question: What is your date of birth?
Answer: I was born on July 12, 1953.

Question: When were you born?
Answer: On July 12, 1953.

Question: What is your birth date?
Answer: My birth date is July 12, 1953.

Question: Where were you born?
Answer: I was born in India.

Question: What is your place of birth?
Answer: I was born in India.

Question: What is your **birth place?**
Answer: I was born in India.

Question: What is your **marital status?**
Answer: I am married.

Question: What is your **marital status?**
Answer: I am divorced.

Question: Are you married?
Answer: No, I am single.

Question: Have you ever been married previously?
Answer: Yes, I was married for one year when I lived in Mexico.

Question: Is your husband a United States citizen?
Answer: No, he is not a United States citizen.

Question: Is your wife a United States citizen?
Answer: Yes, she is.

Question: Why did you get a divorce?
Answer: We fought too much.

Question: How long have you been married?
Answer: I have been married for ten years.

Question: How long have you been a Permanent Resident of the United States?
Answer: I have been a resident for ten years.

Question: When did you first come to the United States?
Answer: I arrived in the United States in 1989.

Question: On what date did you enter the United States?
Answer: I arrived in the United States on September 5, 1989.

Question: How long have you lived in the United States?
Answer: I have lived in the United States for ten years.

Question: Where did you enter the United States?
Answer: I entered the United States in New York City.

Question: What was your **port of entry?**
Answer: JFK airport in New York City.

Question: In what **port of entry** did you arrive in America?
Answer: My port of entry was the Los Angeles airport.

Question: What was your **port of entry?**
Answer: I crossed the United States border near Seattle, Washington.

Question: When did you become a Permanent Resident?
Answer: I became a Permanent Resident in 1990.

Question: In what year did you arrive in the United States?
Answer: I came to America in 1989.

Question: Who is your **employer?**
Answer: I am unemployed right now.

Question: Why aren't you working?
Answer: I was laid off from my last job, and I'm looking for a new job.

Question: Who is your current **employer?**
Answer: My employer is Machines, Inc.

Question: Who do you currently work for?
Answer: I work for Machines, Inc.

Question: Are you currently working?
Answer: Yes, I work for Machines, Inc.

Question: What kind of work do you do?
Answer: I work for Machines, Inc. as a factory worker.

Question: Do you have a job?
Answer: Yes, I work at Machines, Inc.

Question: What is your **occupation?**
Answer: I am a factory worker.

Question: What kind of income do you have?
Answer: I get an income from working for Machines, Inc.

Question: How do you support yourself?
Answer: I work for Machines, Inc.

Question: How long have you held this job?
Answer: I have had this job for three years.

Question: Who was your **employer** before that?
Answer: I used to work for Southwest Airlines.

Question: What job did you have there?
Answer: I worked as a shipping clerk.

Question: How many children do you have?
Answer: I have three children.

Question: Do your children live with you?
Answer: Yes, my children live in my home.

Question: How many people live in your house?
Answer: Five people: myself, my husband, and three children.

Question: Who do you live with?
Answer: I live with my husband and three children.

Question: Where do your children live?
Answer: My children live with me in Brooklyn, New York.

Question: Did any of your children stay in your native country?
Answer: No, all of my children live with me here in Brooklyn.

Question: When were your children **born?**
Answer: One was born in 1992, one in 1994, and one in 1997.

Question: Were they all **born** in the United States?
Answer: Yes, they were born in America.

Question: How many times have you left the United States since you became a Permanent Resident?
Answer: I went out of America only one time.

Question: How long were you away?
Answer: I was gone for three weeks.

Question: Where did you go?
Answer: I went to visit my aunt in Poland.

Question: Why did you leave the United States?
Answer: I wanted to visit my aunt in Poland because she was dying.

Question: Since becoming a Permanent Resident, have you ever left the United States?
Answer: I left only once to go visit my grandmother in Mexico.

Question: When was the last time you left the United States?

Answer: I went to Canada two years ago.

Question: Have you left the United States since you became a Permanent Resident?
Answer: No, I've never left the United States.

Question: Since coming to the U.S., have you traveled to any other country?
Answer: No, I've never left the United States.

Question: Have you visited any other country since becoming a Permanent Resident?
Answer: Yes, I went to Poland to visit my aunt one time.

Question: Have you ever been **deported** by the Immigration office?
Answer: No, I have never been ordered to leave America.

Question: Were you ever ordered to leave the United States?
Answer: No, I have never been **deported.**

Question: Have you ever used a **different** name?
Answer: Yes, my last name used to be Alloutuseth.

Question: Do you want to change your name?
Answer: Yes, I want to change my last name to Allseth.

Question: What other names have you gone by?
Answer: I used to be called Massouleh Alloutuseth.

Question: To what do you want to change your name?
Answer: I want my new name to be Sue Allseth.

Question: What name do you want to have now?
Answer: Sue Allseth.

Question: How do you spell that?
Answer: S-u-e A-l-l-s-e-t-h.

Question: What other names have you used in the past?
Answer: I've never used any other names.

Question: What was your **maiden name?**
Answer: Before I was married, my name was Massouleh Tomei.

Question: What other names have you used in the past?
Answer: Before I was married my name was Massouleh Tomei.

Question: When did you change your name?
Answer: I changed my name ten years ago when I was married.

Question: Why do you want to be an American citizen?
Answer: I want to vote.

Question: Why do you want to be a U.S. citizen?
Answer: I want to travel with a U.S. passport.

Question: Why have you applied for naturalization?
Answer: I want to bring my mother to America.

Question: Were you ever **arrested?**
Answer: Yes, a long time ago.

Question: What were you **arrested** for?
Answer: I stole some money from the corner store.

Question: How about any other arrests?
Answer: No, that was the only time I was arrested.

Question: Have you ever committed any **crime** for which you have not been **arrested?**
Answer: No, I've never done any crimes that I wasn't punished for.

Question: Have you ever been imprisoned for breaking any law?
Answer: I was in jail for three months for robbing the corner store.

Question: When was that?
Answer: During the winter of 1989.

Question: Have you ever failed to file a federal **income tax** return?
Answer: No, I have always filed my taxes.

Question: Have you filed your federal taxes every year?
Answer: Yes, I pay my taxes every year.

Question: Do you pay taxes?
Answer: Yes, I pay federal and state taxes each year.

Question: Was there ever a year when you didn't file your federal tax forms?
Answer: No, I've filed my tax forms every year since I came to America.

Question: Was there ever a year when you didn't file your federal tax forms?
Answer: Yes, I didn't file my first two years in America because I made no money.

Question: Do you pay taxes?
Answer: No, I don't have a job so I don't pay federal income taxes.

Question: Have you ever been a **habitual drunkard?**
Answer: No, I drink only a little.

Question: Were you ever drunk every day?
Answer: No, I drink only one glass of wine a week.

Question: Have you ever advocated or practiced **polygamy?**
Answer: No, I have only one wife.

Question: Have you ever been married to more than one person at a time?
Answer: No, I have always had only one husband.

Question: Have you ever practiced **polygamy?**
Answer: No, I am not married, and I have never been married.

Question: Have you ever been a **prostitute?**
Answer: No, I don't sell my body.

Question: Have you ever been a **prostitute?**
Answer: No, I've never taken money for sex.

Question: Have you ever sold your body for money?
Answer: No, I've never been a **prostitute.**

Question: Have you ever knowingly and for gain helped any alien to enter the U.S. illegally?
Answer: No, I have never **smuggled** anyone into the country.

Question: Have you ever helped someone enter the U.S. illegally?
Answer: No, I have never **smuggled** anyone into the country.

Question: Have you ever **smuggled** anyone into the U.S.?
Answer: No, I have never helped anyone enter America illegally.

Question: Have you ever accepted money for sneaking someone into the U.S.?
Answer: No, I have never helped anyone enter America illegally.

Question: Have you ever been a trafficker in **illegal drugs?**
Answer: No, I have never touched illegal drugs.

Question: Have you ever bought or sold **illegal drugs?**
Answer: No, I am not a drug trafficker.

Question: Have you ever carried **illegal drugs** for someone else?
Answer: No, I have never handled illegal drugs.

Question: Have you ever been a trafficker in cocaine or crack?
Answer: No, I have never sold or carried drugs.

Question: Have you ever bought or sold marijuana or speed?
Answer: No, I have never purchased or sold illegal drugs.

Question: Have you ever received income from **illegal gambling**?
Answer: No, I don't gamble.

Question: Did you ever get money illegally from gambling?
Answer: No, I don't play cards for money.

Question: Have you ever received money from **illegal gambling**?
Answer: No, I don't play cards in anyone's house.

Question: Have you ever received money or other goods from **illegal gambling**?
Answer: No, I don't bet on anything.

Question: Have you ever **claimed** in writing or in any other way to be a U.S. citizen?
Answer: No, I have never lied about my status.

Question: Have you ever **claimed** in writing or in any other way to be a U.S. citizen?
Answer: No, I never said I was a U.S. citizen.

Question: Have you ever pretended to be a U.S. citizen?
Answer: No, I have never lied about my citizenship.

Question: Have you ever **claimed** in writing to be a U.S. citizen?
Answer: No, I have never pretended to be an American citizen.

Question: Have you ever **claimed** in writing or in any other way to be a U.S. citizen?
Answer: No, I am not a U.S. citizen.

Question: Have you ever voted or **registered** to vote in the United States?
Answer: No, I have never tried to vote because I am not a U.S. citizen.

Question: Have you ever voted or **registered** to vote in the United States?
Answer: No, I am not a U.S. citizen.

Question: Have you ever voted or **registered** to vote in the United States?
Answer: No, I have never tried to vote in America.

Question: Do you believe in the **Constitution** and the government of the United States?
Answer: Yes, I think the **Constitution** is a good law.

Question: Do you believe in the **Constitution** of the United States?
Answer: Yes, I want to follow the **Constitution**.

Question: Do you believe in the government of the United States?
Answer: Yes, I think the government is very good.

Question: Do you believe in the **Constitution** and the government of the United States?
Answer: Yes, I believe that the **Constitution** is a good law.

Question: Are you willing to take the full **Oath of Allegiance** to the United States?
Answer: Yes, I am ready to help my new country.

Question: Are you willing to take the full **Oath of Allegiance** to the United States?
Answer: Yes, I promise to help my new country. I can't help my old country.

Question: Are you willing to take the full **Oath of Allegiance** to the United States?
Answer: Yes, I want to do what is best for America.

Question: Are you willing to take the full **Oath of Allegiance** to the United States?
Answer: Yes, I want to officially swear to help the United States.

Question: Have you ever been declared legally **incompetent** or confined as a patient in a **mental institution**?
Answer: No, I am not crazy.

Question: Were you ever in a mental hospital?
Answer: No, I am mentally competent.

Question: Have you ever been confined as a patient in a **mental institution?**
Answer: No, I've never been in a hospital for people whose minds don't work right.

Question: Were you born with or have you acquired any title of **nobility?**
Answer: No, my parents were factory workers.

Question: Are you a king, queen, duke, earl, prince, or do you have any other title of **nobility?**
Answer: No, I don't have any special titles along with my name and I am not a king or any other noble.

Question: Were you born with or have you acquired any title of **nobility?**
Answer: No, no one in my family is related to a king or queen.

Question: Have you at any time ever ordered, incited, assisted, or otherwise participated in the **persecution** of any person because of race, religion, national origin, or political opinion?
Answer: No, I have never hurt anyone.

Question: Have you at any time ever ordered or otherwise participated in the **persecution** of any person because of race, religion, national origin, or political opinion?
Answer: No, I don't hurt people because of what they believe or what color they are.

Question: Have you ever participated in the **persecution** of any person because of race, religion, national origin, or political opinion?
Answer: No, I have never persecuted anyone.

Question: If the law requires it, are you willing to perform **noncombatant services** in the Armed Forces of the United States?
Answer: Yes, I will help the soldiers when the law tells me.

Question: If required by law, are you willing to perform **noncombatant** services in the Armed Forces of the United States?

Answer: Yes, I will do whatever I can to help the military.

Question: Are you willing to perform **noncombatant services** in the Armed Forces of the United States, if the law says you must?

Answer: Yes, I will help the Armed Forces if the law tells me.

Question: If the law requires it, are you willing to perform work of **national importance** under civilian direction?

Answer: Yes, I will do anything to help the United States when the law says I must.

Question: Are you willing to perform work of **national importance** under civilian direction, if required by the law?

Answer: Yes, if the law tells me, I will work to help the United States.

Question: Will you perform work of **national importance** under civilian direction, when the law says you must?

Answer: Yes, I will do anything to help the United States whenever it is needed.

Question: Have you ever left the United States to avoid being **drafted** into the U.S. Armed Forces?

Answer: No, I have never gone away to avoid going into the military.

Question: Have you ever left the United States to avoid being **drafted?**

Answer: No, I have never left the country so I didn't have to go to war.

Question: Have you ever left the United States so you didn't have to fight in a war?

Answer: No, I have never gone away to avoid being drafted into the military.

Question: Have you ever failed to comply with Selective Service laws?

Answer: No, I never withheld my name for becoming a soldier.

Question: Have you ever failed to comply with Selective Service laws?

Answer: No, I have always given my name so I could be called to fight.

Question: Did you register for the Selective Service?

Answer: Yes, I gave my name to the government.

Question: Do you know your Selective Service number?
Answer: Yes, I have that number written on this paper.

Question: Did you ever apply for **exemption** from military service because of **alienage, conscientious objections,** or other reasons?
Answer: No, I have never said that I would not fight for America.

Question: Have you ever tried to avoid military service?
Answer: No, I have always been willing to be a soldier.

Question: Did you ever request to stay out of the Armed Forces because of your religious beliefs?
Answer: No, my religion says it is okay to protect my country by fighting a war.

Question: Have you ever **deserted** from the military, air, or naval forces of the United States?
Answer: No, I have never even been in the Armed Forces.

Question: Have you ever **deserted** from the military, air, or naval forces of the United States?
Answer: No, I was honorably discharged from the army.

Question: Did you leave the Armed Forces before you were allowed to?
Answer: No, I was in the Armed Forces for a full three years.

Question: Are you a member of the **Communist** Party?
Answer: No, I am not a member of any group.

Question: Have you ever been a member of the **Communist** Party?
Answer: No, I never joined that group.

Question: Are you now or have you ever been a member of the **Communist** Party?
Answer: I am not a member now, but I was many years ago.

Question: Why were you a **Communist?**
Answer: I joined because everyone else joined. I didn't believe in it.

Question: When was that?
Answer: I joined in 1972, but I never went to the meetings.

Question: Have you ever been **affiliated** with the Nazi Party?
Answer: No, I don't agree with the Nazi Party.

Question: Have you ever been a member of the Nazi Party?
Answer: No, I never joined the Nazi Party.

Question: Did you help the Nazi government in any way?
Answer: No, I never assisted the Nazis.

Question: Were you a part of the Nazi Party between 1933 and 1945?
Answer: No, I don't agree with the Nazi Party.

Question: Have you ever helped the Nazi Party?
Answer: No, I don't like the Nazi Party.

Question: Are you a member of any clubs or organizations?
Answer: No, I am not a part of any organized groups.

Question: Are you a member of any clubs or organizations?
Answer: Yes, I am a member of the Small Business Association.

Question: Are you a member of any clubs?
Answer: No, I do not take part in any clubs.

Question: Have you ever given **false testimony** to obtain an immigration benefit?
Answer: No, I have never lied.

Question: Have you ever lied to obtain an immigration benefit?
Answer: No, I have never given **false testimony.**

Question: Have you ever lied at an immigration interview when you were under **oath?**

Answer: No, I have never lied after swearing to tell the truth.

Question: If the law requires it, are you willing to **bear arms** on behalf of the United States?

Answer: Yes, I will fight in a war to help the United States.

Question: If the law requires it, are you willing to **bear arms** on behalf of the United States?

Answer: Yes, I will be a soldier if the law tells me.

Question: Are you willing to **bear arms** for the United States, even if it is against the country you used to live in?

Answer: Yes, I will fight for America even if it is against my old country.

CHAPTER 8

Sample Dictation Sentences

Here are sample sentences you may be asked to write down during your INS interview. These dictation sentences have previously appeared in the lessons in Chapter 4. Practice writing each sentence on the page opposite it. Have your partner read the sentence out loud to you and then write it down carefully.

1. I study.

2. I study English.

3. I study citizenship.

4. I want to be a citizen.

5. I want to be an American.

6. I live in California.

7. I live with my family.

8. I live in California with my family.

9. I want to be an American citizen.

10. I want to be a citizen of the United States.

11. I drive to work.

12. I drive my car to work.

13. I like to drive my car to work.

14. I take the bus.

15. I take the bus to work.

16. I like to take the bus.

17. I go to school.

18. My children go to school.

1. _____

2. _____

3. _____

4. _____

5. _____

6. _____

7. _____

8. _____

9. _____

10. _____

11. _____

12. _____

13. _____

14. _____

15. _____

16. _____

17. _____

18. _____

19. My children and I go to school.

20. The little girl is happy.

21. My family is happy to be in America.

22. The little girl and my family are happy.

23. I believe in freedom.

24. I believe in the Constitution.

25. I believe in freedom and the Constitution.

26. The sky is blue.

27. My dog is brown.

28. The sky is blue and my dog is brown.

29. There is a bird.

30. The bird is in the tree.

31. There is a bird in the tree.

32. I have four children.

33. I live with my children.

34. I live with my four children.

35. I drive a car.

36. I drive a big red car.

19. _____

20. _____

21. _____

22. _____

23. _____

24. _____

25. _____

26. _____

27. _____

28. _____

29. _____

30. _____

31. _____

32. _____

33. _____

34. _____

35. _____

36. _____

37. I like my car.

38. I live in a house.

39. I live in a blue house.

40. I like my house.

41. The woman eats.

42. The woman eats food.

43. The woman eats two apples.

44. I have a cat.

45. I have a small cat.

46. I like cats.

47. I wear a hat.

48. I wear a yellow hat.

49. I wear hats.

50. I am learning English.

51. They are learning English.

52. My sisters are learning English.

53. I like snow.

54. Today it is snowing.

37. _____

38. _____

39. _____

40. _____

41. _____

42. _____

43. _____

44. _____

45. _____

46. _____

47. _____

48. _____

49. _____

50. _____

51. _____

52. _____

53. _____

54. _____

55. The snow is cold.

56. The child plays.

57. The child plays with a toy.

58. The child likes the toy.

59. I can read English.

60. I can write English.

61. I can read, write, and speak English.

62. Today is Tuesday.

63. Tomorrow is Wednesday.

64. Today it is windy.

65. It is cold.

66. It is cold outside.

67. I like cold weather.

55. _____

56. _____

57. _____

58. _____

59. _____

60. _____

61. _____

62. _____

63. _____

64. _____

65. _____

66. _____

67. _____

APPENDIX A

Answers to Chapter 4 Exercises

ANSWERS TO LESSON 1

Answers to Test Questions

1. C. President, Vice President, Cabinet
2. A. Congress
3. B. Supreme Court
4. B. executive, judicial, legislative
5. C. three

Circled Answers

1. What is the judicial branch?   Congress   (Supreme Court)

2. How many branches of government are there?   five   (three)

3. What is the executive branch?   Supreme Court   (President, Cabinet Vice President)

4. What is the legislative branch?   (Congress)   President

5. What are the three branches of government?   federal, state, judicial   (executive, judicial, legislative)

Yes or No Answers

Yes (No) The President is in the judicial branch of government.

(Yes) No The Supreme Court is in the judicial branch of government.

(Yes) No There are three branches of government.

Yes (No) The Congress is in the executive branch of government.

(Yes) No The President is in the executive branch of government.

Yes (No) There are five branches of government.

ANSWERS TO LESSON 2

Answers to Test Questions

1. D. Congress

2. B. makes laws

3. C. Senate and House of Representatives

4. D. in the Capitol in Washington, DC

5. C. the people

6. A. the place where Congress meets

7. B. Congress

Matching Answers

__C__ Who elects Congress?

__E__ Who makes the laws in the United States?

__D__ What is Congress?

__B__ What are the duties of Congress?

__A__ Where does Congress meet?

__F__ What does Congress have the power to declare?

A. the Capitol in Washington, DC

B. to make laws

C. the people

D. Senate and House of Representatives

E. Congress

F. war

Yes or No Answers

Ⓨes   No   Congress makes the laws in the United States.

Yes   Ⓝo   The President has the power to declare war.

Ⓨes   No   Congress includes the Senate and the House of Representatives.

Yes   Ⓝo   The duties of Congress are to please the people.

Ⓨes   No   The duties of Congress are to make laws.

Yes   Ⓝo   Congress meets in New York City.

Ⓨes   No   Congress has the power to declare war.

ANSWERS TO LESSON 3

Answers to Test Questions

1. B. there are two senators from each state

2. D. no limit

3. B. 100

4. C. six

Circled Answers

1. There are _____ senators in Congress.   ⓐ00   435

2. A senator is elected for _____ years.   ⓢix   ten

3. How many times can a senator be re-elected?   Ⓝo limit   ten

4. There are 100 senators because there are _____.   ⓣwo from each state   four from each state

5. The word "union" means _____.   ⓣhe United States   provinces in Canada

Yes or No Answers

Yes   Ⓝo   A senator is elected for 100 years.

Ⓨes   No   There are 100 senators because there are two from each state.

Ⓨes   No   There is no limit to how many times a senator can be re-elected.

Ⓨes   No   A senator is elected for six years.

Yes   Ⓝo   There are 435 senators in Congress.

ANSWERS TO LESSON 4

Answers to Test Questions

1. B. two years
2. D. no limit
3. C. 435
4. A. two

Filled-In Blanks

1. There are <u>435</u> representatives in Congress.

2. A representative is elected for <u>two</u> years.

3. There is <u>no limit</u> to the number of times a representative can be re-elected.

4. If there are many people in a state, they can elect <u>many</u> representatives.

Yes or No Answers

(Yes) No   A representative is elected for a two-year term.

Yes (No)   There are 435 representatives because there are two from each state.

(Yes) No   There is no limit to how many times a representative can be re-elected.

(Yes) No   A representative is elected for two years.

(Yes) No   There are 435 representatives in Congress.

Answers to Review Test 1

1. C. three
2. A. Congress
3. D. Supreme Court
4. A. President, Vice President, Cabinet
5. B. executive, legislative, judicial
6. B. Capitol in Washington, DC
7. B. Senate and House of Representatives
8. D. the people
9. C. Congress
10. A. to make laws
11. A. two from each state
12. C. no limit
13. C. six years
14. A. 100
15. B. 435

ANSWERS TO LESSON 5

Answers to Test Questions

1. B. nine
2. C. the President
3. C. to interpret laws
4. D. William Rehnquist
5. A. Supreme Court

Filled-In Blanks

1. The <u>President</u> selects the Supreme Court justices.

2. The duty of the Supreme Court is to <u>interpret</u> laws.

3. The <u>Supreme</u> Court is the highest court in the United States.

4. There are <u>nine</u> justices on the Supreme Court.

5. William <u>Rehnquist</u> is the chief justice of the Supreme Court.

Yes or No Answers

Yes **(No)** The duty of the Supreme Court is to make laws.
(Yes) No The duty of the Supreme Court is to interpret laws.
(Yes) No There are nine justices on the Supreme Court.
Yes **(No)** William Rehnquist is the Vice President.
(Yes) No The President appoints the Supreme Court justices.

ANSWERS TO LESSON 6

Answers to Test Questions

1. C. Electoral College
2. D. George Washington
3. A. to enforce laws
4. D. four years
5. A. Al Gore

Matching Answers

__E__	first President of the United States	A. four years
__D__	Vice President	B. Bill Clinton
__A__	how long the President is elected	C. Electoral College
__B__	President today	D. Al Gore
__C__	elects the President	E. George Washington
__F__	duty of executive branch	F. enforce the law

Yes or No Answers

(Yes)   No   The duty of the executive branch is to enforce laws.

Yes   (No)   The duty of the executive branch is to interpret laws.

(Yes)   No   George Washington was the first President of the United States.

Yes   (No)   Bill Clinton is the Vice President today.

(Yes)   No   The President is elected by the Electoral College.

(Yes)   No   The President is elected for four years.

ANSWERS TO LESSON 7

Answers to Test Questions

1. B. two
2. A. Vice President
3. D. Cabinet
4. D. Speaker of the House of Representatives
5. B. thirty-five years old

Circled Answers

1. What is one requirement to be President?   born in Canada   (natural born citizen of the U.S.)

2. Who becomes President if the President dies?   First Lady   (Vice President)

3. What special group advises the President?   Congress   (Cabinet)

4. Who becomes President if the President and Vice President die   (Speaker of the House of Representatives)   Congress

5. How many terms can a President serve?   (two)   three

Yes or No Answers

(Yes) No   To become President, you must be a natural born citizen of the U.S.

(Yes) No   The Cabinet advises the President.

(Yes) No   The duty of the executive branch is to enforce laws.

Yes (No)   The First Lady becomes President if the President dies.

(Yes) No   The executive branch of the government includes the President, Vice President, and Cabinet.

(Yes) No   The President can serve two terms in office.

Yes (No)   To become President, you must be at least fifty years old.

Answers to Review Test 2

1. D. no limit
2. A. two years
3. A. 435
4. C. interpret laws
5. A. William Rehnquist
6. A. President
7. D. nine
8. A. Supreme Court
9. C. four years
10. B. Electoral College
11. B. Al Gore
12. A. Bill Clinton
13. C. George Washington
14. C. enforce laws

ANSWERS TO LESSON 8

Answers to Test Questions

1. B. November
2. D. January
3. B. White House
4. A. Washington, DC
5. C. we vote for the President

Matching Answers

__B__ the President's official home   A. January

__D__ we vote for the President during this month   B. White House

__A__ the President is inaugurated during this month   C. Washington, DC

__C__ the White House is located here   D. November

Yes or No Answers

Yes	**No**	The White House is located in Philadelphia, PA.
Yes	No	The White House is the President's official home.
Yes	**No**	The President is inaugurated in November.
Yes	**No**	We vote for the President in January.
Yes	**No**	The Cabinet is the President's official home.
Yes	No	The White House is located in Washington, DC.
Yes	No	The President is inaugurated in January.
Yes	No	We vote for the President in November.

ANSWERS TO LESSON 9

Answers to Test Questions

1. A. President
2. D. George Washington
3. C. mayor
4. B. governor
5. B. Bill Clinton

Filled-In Blanks

1. The <u>President</u> signs a bill into law.

2. The head executive of a city government is the <u>mayor</u>.

3. The <u>President</u> is commander in chief of the U.S. military.

4. The <u>governor</u> is head executive of a state government.

5. The first commander in chief of the U.S. military was <u>George Washington</u>.

Yes or No Answers

Yes	**No**	The governor is the head executive of a city government.
Yes	No	The President signs a bill into law.
Yes	No	George Washington was the first commander in chief of the U.S. military.
Yes	No	The mayor is the head executive of a city government.
Yes	No	Bill Clinton is the commander in chief of the U.S. military today.
Yes	No	The President is the head executive of the United States.
Yes	**No**	The mayor is the head executive of a state government.

Answers to Review Test 3

1. C. Speaker of the House of Representatives
2. A. two
3. A. Vice President
4. A. natural born citizen of the U.S.
5. B. Cabinet
6. D. George Washington
7. B. Bill Clinton
8. A. White House
9. D. President
10. A. mayor
11. C. governor
12. B. President's official home
13. A. Washington, DC
14. D. November
15. D. January

ANSWERS TO LESSON 10

Answers to Test Questions

1. C. Constitution
2. B. amendment
3. B. 1787
4. A. the supreme law of the land
5. D. twenty-seven

Filled-In Blanks

1. There are <u>twenty-seven</u> amendments to the Constitution.

2. A change to the Constitution is an <u>amendment</u>.

3. The Constitution is the supreme <u>law</u> of the land.

4. <u>Yes</u>, the Constitution can be changed.

5. The supreme law of the land is the <u>Constitution</u>.

6. The Constitution was written in <u>1787</u>.

Yes or No Answers

(Yes) No   The Constitution is the supreme law of the land.

(Yes) No   A change to the Constitution is called an amendment.

Yes (No)   The Constitution cannot be changed.

Yes (No)   The Constitution was written in 1776.

(Yes) No   The supreme law of the land is the Constitution.

(Yes) No   There are twenty-seven amendments to the Constitution.

(Yes) No   The Constitution was written in 1787.

Yes (No)   There are twenty-four amendments to the Constitution.

ANSWERS TO LESSON 11

Answers to Test Questions

1. C. Bill of Rights
2. D. first ten amendments to the Constitution
3. A. Bill of Rights
4. D. everyone in America, including non-citizens
5. A. preamble

Circled Answers

1. the first ten amendments   (Bill of Rights)   Congress

2. the introduction to the Constitution (preamble)   Bill of Rights

3. freedom of speech comes from here   President   (Bill of Rights)

4. the Constitution guarantees these   only citizens   (everyone)
   people rights

5. the Bill of Rights   (first ten   Supreme Court
                                        amendments)

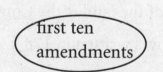

Yes or No Answers

(Yes) No   The Constitution is the supreme law of the land.

(Yes) No   The first ten amendments to the Constitution are called the Bill of Rights.

(Yes) No   Freedom of speech comes from the Bill of Rights.

Yes (No)   The Bill of Rights is the first twelve amendments to the Constitution.

(Yes) No   The introduction to the Constitution is called the preamble.

(Yes) No   Everyone is protected by the Bill of Rights, including non-citizens.

(Yes) No   The Bill of Rights is the first ten amendments to the Constitution.

Yes (No)   The conclusion to the Constitution is called the preamble.

ANSWERS TO LESSON 12

Answers to Test Questions

1. C. Bill of Rights

2. B. right to bear arms

3. D. government may not put soldiers in people's homes

4. A. a person may not be tried for the same crime twice

5. B. freedom of speech

List of Correct Answers

1. The freedom of speech, press, and religion

2. Right to bear arms

3. Government may not put soldiers in people's homes

4. Government may not search or take a person's property without a warrant

5. A person may not be tried for the same crime twice

6. A person charged with a crime has rights including the right to a trial and a lawyer

7. People are protected from unreasonable fines or cruel punishment

Yes or No Answers

(Yes) No The Constitution is the supreme law of the land.

(Yes) No The first ten amendments to the Constitution are called the Bill of Rights.

(Yes) No Freedom of speech comes from the Bill of Rights.

(Yes) No The right to bear arms comes from the Bill of Rights.

(Yes) No Everyone is protected by the Bill of Rights, including non-citizens.

(Yes) No The government may not search or take a person's property without a warrant.

(Yes) No The Bill of Rights is the first ten amendments to the Constitution.

(Yes) No A person in America may not be tried for the same crime twice.

Yes (No) People in America are not protected from unreasonable fines.

(Yes) No Freedom of religion comes from the Bill of Rights.

(Yes) No The government may not put soldiers in people's homes.

Answers to Review Test 4

1. A. 1787
2. B. Constitution
3. D. twenty-seven
4. A. amendment
5. B. yes
6. A. supreme law of the land

7. C. Bill of Rights
8. D. both citizens and non-citizens
9. D. preamble
10. C. Bill of Rights
11. A. first ten amendments
12. A. freedom of speech

ANSWERS TO LESSON 13

Answers to Test Questions

1. A. Native Americans
2. C. religious freedom
3. D. Mayflower
4. A. Thanksgiving
5. B. Native Americans

Matching Answers

__D__ ship that brought the pilgrims to   A. Thanksgiving
America

__C__ helped the pilgrims in America   B. religious freedom

__A__ holiday celebrated by the American   C. Native Americans
colonists

__B__ reason pilgrims came to America   D. Mayflower

Yes or No Answers

(Yes) No   The Native Americans helped the pilgrims.
Yes   (No)   The pilgrims came to America because they wanted a vacation.
Yes   (No)   The pilgrims came to America on a ship called the Titanic.
(Yes) No   Thanksgiving was the first holiday celebrated by the pilgrims.
(Yes) No   The pilgrims were the first American colonists.
(Yes) No   The pilgrims came to America for religious freedom.
Yes   (No)   Easter was the first holiday celebrated by the pilgrims.
(Yes) No   A ship called the Mayflower brought the pilgrims to America.

ANSWERS TO LESSON 14

Answers to Test Questions

1. B. colonies
2. A. Connecticut
3. B. New York
4. A. Virginia
5. A. Maryland

Filled-In Blanks

The original thirteen states were called the <u>colonies</u>.
Name two of the original thirteen states: <u>Connecticut</u> and <u>New Hampshire</u>.
Name two more of the original thirteen states: <u>New York</u> and <u>New Jersey</u>.

Yes or No Answers

(Yes)	No	The thirteen original states were called the colonies.
(Yes)	No	New York was one of the colonies.
Yes	(No)	Texas was one of the colonies.
Yes	(No)	The thirteen original states were called the settlements.
(Yes)	No	Connecticut was one of the original thirteen states.
Yes	(No)	California was one of the original thirteen states.
(Yes)	No	Georgia was one of the colonies.
(Yes)	No	Maryland was one of the original thirteen states.

ANSWERS TO LESSON 15

Answers to Test Questions

1. A. 1776
2. B. all men are created equal
3. C. Thomas Jefferson
4. D. July 4th
5. D. Independence Day

Filled-In Blanks

1. The Declaration of Independence was adopted on <u>July 4</u>, 1776.

2. The basic belief of the Declaration of Independence is <u>all men are created equal</u>.

3. <u>Independence</u> Day is on the 4th of July.

4. The main writer of the Declaration of Independence was <u>Thomas Jefferson</u>.

5. Independence Day is on July <u>4th</u>.

Yes or No Answers

  (Yes)   No   The 4th of July is Independence Day.

  (Yes)   No   The basic belief of the Declaration of Independence is that all men are created equal.

  (Yes)   No   The Declaration of Independence was adopted in 1776.

  Yes   (No)   The main writer of the Declaration of Independence was George Washington.

  Yes   (No)   The basic belief of the Declaration of Independence is that the people should work seven days a week.

  Yes   (No)   The Declaration of Independence was written in 1787.

  Yes   (No)   The basic belief of the Declaration of Independence is that the President should have absolute power.

  (Yes)   No   The Declaration of Independence was adopted on July 4, 1776.

  (Yes)   No   The main writer of the Declaration of Independence was Thomas Jefferson.

  Yes   (No)   Independence Day is on December 25th.

Answers to Review Test 5

1. B. religious freedom
2. C. Mayflower
3. D. Thanksgiving
4. A. Native Americans
5. D. Thomas Jefferson
6. B. July 4, 1776
7. C. all men are created equal
8. A. colonies
9. D. New York

ANSWERS TO LESSON 16

Answers to Test Questions

1. A. England
2. B. George Washington
3. C. George Washington
4. B. Patrick Henry
5. A. George Washington
6. C. England

Filled-In Blanks

1. <u>George Washington</u> was the first commander in chief of the U.S. military.

2. Patrick <u>Henry</u> said, "Give me liberty or give me death."

3. The U.S. gained independence from <u>England</u>.

4. The United States fought <u>England</u> during the Revolutionary War.

5. <u>George Washington</u> was the first President elected by the people in the United States.

6. George Washington is called the "father of our <u>country</u>."

Yes or No Questions

(Yes)	No	George Washington was the first commander in chief of the U.S. military.
Yes	(No)	America fought France during the Revolutionary War.
Yes	(No)	Thomas Jefferson said, "Give me liberty or give me death."
(Yes)	No	The U.S. gained independence from England.
(Yes)	No	George Washington is called the "father of our country."
Yes	(No)	Patrick Henry said, "Give me life or freedom."
(Yes)	No	America fought England during the Revolutionary War.
(Yes)	No	Patrick Henry said, "Give me liberty or give me death."
(Yes)	No	George Washington was the first President elected by the people in the United States.

ANSWERS TO LESSON 17

Answers to Test Questions

1. B. the North
2. C. slavery
3. D. North and South
4. A. the South
5. B. the North

Filled-In Answers

1. <u>The South</u> wanted to start their own country.

2. During the Civil War the <u>North/South</u> fought.

3. <u>Slavery</u> was one reason for the Civil War.

4. The North wanted the states to stay <u>together</u>.

5. The <u>North</u> won the Civil War.

Yes or No Questions

Yes (No)   The East and West fought during the Civil War.
(Yes) No   The South wanted to start their own country.
Yes (No)   The South won the Civil War.
(Yes) No   The North wanted the states to stay together.
(Yes) No   The North and South fought during the Civil War.
(Yes) No   One reason for the Civil War was slavery.
(Yes) No   The North won the Civil War.

ANSWERS TO LESSON 18

Answers to Test Questions

1. A. President Lincoln
2. A. Abraham Lincoln
3. A. freed the slaves
4. B. the Emancipation Proclamation

Filled-In Blanks

1. President <u>Lincoln</u> freed the slaves.

2. Abraham <u>Lincoln</u> was President during the Civil War.

3. The Emancipation Proclamation freed the <u>slaves</u>.

4. The <u>North</u> won the Civil War.

Yes or No Answers

Yes (No)   George Washington was President during the Civil War.

(Yes) No   President Lincoln freed the slaves.

(Yes) No   The Emancipation Proclamation freed the slaves.

(Yes) No   Abraham Lincoln was President during the Civil War.

(Yes) No   The slaves were freed by the Emancipation Proclamation.

(Yes) No   The North won the Civil War.

ANSWERS TO LESSON 19

Answers to Test Questions

1. B. for countries to talk about world problems and try to solve them

2. D. Alaska

3. A. Germany, Italy, and Japan

4. C. Hawaii

5. A. civil rights leader

6. C. Britain, Canada, Australia, New Zealand, Russia, China, and France

7. A. Alaska and Hawaii

Circled Answers

1. Who were two of America's enemies in World War II?   Britain/Canada   (Japan/Italy)

2. Who were two of America's allies in World War II?   (Britain/Canada)   Japan/Italy

3. Where do countries talk about world problems and try to solve them?   (United Nations)   United Justices

4. What was the 49th state to join the union?   (Alaska)   Connecticut

5. What was the 50th state to join the union?   Utah   (Hawaii)

6. Who was a civil rights leader?   (Martin Luther King, Jr.)   Francis Scott Key

Yes or No Answers

(Yes) No   Germany and Japan were two of America's enemies in World War II.

(Yes) No   China and Britain were two of America's allies in World War II.

(Yes) No   Countries talk about world problems and try to solve them at the United Nations.

Yes (No)   Wyoming was the 49th state to join the union.

(Yes) No   Hawaii was the 50th state to join the union.

(Yes) No   Martin Luther King, Jr. was a civil rights leader.

(Yes) No   Russia and France were two of America's allies in World War II.

Yes (No)   Martin Luther King, Jr. was a congressman.

ANSWERS TO LESSON 20

Answers to Test Questions

1. B. Washington, DC
2. A. Democratic Republic
3. C. fifty
4. A. Democrat and Republican

Filled-In Blanks

1. Democrat and Republican are the two major <u>political parties</u> in the United States.

2. There are <u>fifty</u> states in America.

3. <u>Democrat</u> and Republican are the two major political parties in the United States.

4. The United States has a Democratic <u>Republic</u> form of government.

5. The capital of the United States is in <u>Washington, DC</u>.

Yes or No Answers

Yes (No)   The capital of the United States is in New York City.

(Yes) No   The United States has a Democratic Republic form of government.

(Yes) No   There are fifty states in America.

(Yes) No   Democrat and Republican are the two major political parties in the United States.

Yes (No)   The United States has a Communist form of government.

(Yes) No   The capital of the United States is in Washington, DC.

(Yes) No   The United States is made up of fifty states.

ANSWERS TO LESSON 21

Answers to Test Questions

1. C. fifty

2. A. red, white, blue

3. B. thirteen

4. B. white

5. B. original thirteen colonies

6. A. fifty states

7. A. red and white

8. A. The Star-Spangled Banner

9. C. Francis Scott Key

Matching Answers

_H_	What do the stripes on the flag represent?	A. red, white, blue
_G_	What color are the stripes?	B. fifty
_F_	Who wrote "The Star-Spangled Banner"?	C. white
_C_	What color are the stars on the flag?	D. fifty states
_E_	How many stripes are on the flag?	E. thirteen
_D_	What do the stars on the flag represent?	F. Francis Scott Key
_A_	What are the colors of our flag?	G. red and white
_B_	How many stars are on the flag?	H. original thirteen colonies
_I_	What is the national anthem of the United States?	I. "The Star-Spangled Banner"

Yes or No Answers

(Yes) No   The stars on the flag are white.

(Yes) No   The flag is red, white, and blue.

(Yes) No   The stripes on the flag represent the original thirteen colonies.

Yes (No)   The flag has twelve stripes on it.

(Yes) No   Francis Scott Key wrote "The Star-Spangled Banner."

(Yes) No   The stripes on the flag are red and white.

Yes (No)   The stars on the flag represent the fifty stars in the sky.

Yes (No)   The stars on the flag are blue.

(Yes) No   "The Star-Spangled Banner" is the national anthem of the United States.

(Yes) No   The flag has fifty stars on it.

ANSWERS TO LESSON 22

Ask a teacher, friend, or relative the answers to the following questions. If you can't find the answer to one of these questions, go to your local public library and ask the librarian. Write in the answers that you find.

1. The head of your local government is _____.

2. _____ is the capital of your state.

3. The governor of your state is _____.

4. The two senators from your state are _____ and _____.

5. _____ is the mayor of your city.

ANSWERS TO LESSON 23

Answers to Test Questions

1. B. right to vote
2. D. fifteenth
3. B. eighteen
4. D. right to vote
5. B. N-400 "Application for Naturalization"

Circled Answers

1. Which amendment to the Constitution guarantees or discusses voting rights?   third   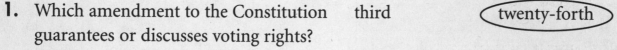 twenty-forth

2. What is the most important right granted to U.S. citizens?   right to vote   right to work

3. What is the minimum voting age in the United States?   sixteen   eighteen

4. What is a benefit of becoming a U.S. citizen?   right to travel with a U.S. passport   right to own a home

5. What INS form is used to apply to become a naturalized citizen?   N-400 "Application for Naturalization"   N-200 "Petition for Naturalization"

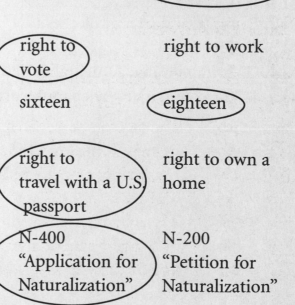

Yes or No Answers

Yes ~~No~~   The minimum voting age in the United States is twenty-one.

~~Yes~~ No   The right to vote is the most important right granted to U.S. citizens.

~~Yes~~ No   The right to travel with a U.S. passport is granted to U.S. citizens.

~~Yes~~ No   The 15th, 19th, 24th, and 26th amendments to the Constitution guarantee or discuss voting rights.

Yes ~~No~~   The right to bear arms is the most important right granted to U.S. citizens.

~~Yes~~ No   The N-400 "Application for Naturalization" is the INS form you use to apply to become a U.S. citizen.

~~Yes~~ No   Eighteen is the minimum voting age in the United States.

Answers to Review Test 6

1. B. two
2. D. Germany, Italy, Japan
3. C. civil rights leader
4. D. Alaska and Hawaii
5. D. eighteen
6. A. right to vote
7. C. fifty
8. B. Democrat and Republican
9. A. Democratic Republic
10. A. red, white, blue
11. B. thirteen
12. B. original thirteen colonies
13. A. fifty states
14. C. Britain, Canada, Australia, New Zealand, Russia, China, and France
15. B. for countries to talk about world problems and try to solve them

APPENDIX B

SAMPLE N-400 APPLICATION

This appendix contains a copy of the N-400 "Application for Naturalization." You can practice filling it out, but this is not the real application. You can get the real application from an INS office near you. Remember that INS changes the N-400 from time to time, so the one you fill out might look a bit different from the one in this appendix.

U.S. Department of Justice
Immigration and Naturalization Service

OMB #1115-0009
Application for Naturalization

START HERE - Please Type or Print

Part 1.   Information about you.

Family Name	Given Name	Middle Initial

U.S. Mailing Address - Care of

Street Number and Name		Apt. #
City	County	
State	ZIP Code	
Date of Birth (month/day/year)	Country of Birth	
Social Security #	A #	

Part 2.   Basis for Eligibility (check one).

a. ☐ I have been a permanent resident for at least five (5) years.

b. ☐ I have been a permanent resident for at least three (3) years and have been married to a United States Citizen for those three years.

c. ☐ I am a permanent resident child of United States citizen parent(s).

d. ☐ I am applying on the basis of qualifying military service in the Armed Forces of the U.S. and have attached completed Forms N-426 and G-325B

e. ☐ Other. (Please specify section of law) _____

Part 3.   Additional information about you.

Date you became a permanent resident (month/day/year)	Port admitted with an immmigrant visa or INS Office where granted adjustment of status.

Citizenship

Name on alien registration card (if different than in Part 1)

Other names used since you became a permanent resident (including maiden name)

Sex ☐ Male ☐ Female	Height	Marital Status: ☐ Single ☐ Married ☐ Divorced ☐ Widowed

Can you speak, read and write English ?   ☐No ☐Yes.

Absences from the U.S.:

Have you been absent from the U.S. since becoming a permanent resident?   ☐ No ☐Yes.

If you answered **"Yes"**, complete the following. Begin with your most recent absence. If you need more room to explain the reason for an absence or to list more trips, continue on separate paper.

Date left U.S.	Date returned	Did absence last 6 months or more?		Destination	Reason for trip
		Yes	No		
		Yes	No		
		Yes	No		
		Yes	No		
		Yes	No		
		Yes	No		

Form N-400 (Rev. 07/17/91)N Internet

Continued on back.

FOR INS USE ONLY

Returned	Receipt

Resubmitted

Reloc Sent

Reloc Rec'd

☐ Applicant Interviewed

At interview
☐ request naturalization ceremony at court

Remarks

Action

To Be Completed by
Attorney or *Representative*, if any
Fill in box if G-28 is attached to represent the applicant

VOLAG#

ATTY State License #

Part 4. Information about your residences and employment.

List your addresses during the last five (5) years or since you became a permanent resident, whichever is less. Begin with your current address. If you need more space, continue on separate paper.

Street Number and Name, City, State, Country, and Zip Code	Dates (month/day/year)	
	From	To

List your employers during the last five (5) years. List your present or most recent employer first. If none, write "None". If you need more space, continue on separate paper.

Employer's Name	Employer's Address		Dates Employed (month/day/year)		Occupation/position
	Street Name and Number - City, State and ZIP Code		From	To	

Part 5. Information about your marital history.

A. Total number of times you have been married _____ . If you are now married, complete the following regarding your husband or wife.

Family name	Given name	Middle initial
Address		

Date of birth (month/day/year)	Country of birth	Citizenship
Social Security#	A# *(if applicable)*	Immigration status (If not a U.S. citizen)

Naturalization (If applicable)
(month/day/year)   Place   (City, State)

If you have ever previously been married or if your current spouse has been previously married, please provide the following on separate paper: Name of prior spouse, date of marriage, date marriage ended, how marriage ended and immigration status of prior spouse.

Part 6. Information about your children.

Total Number of Children _____ . Complete the following information for each of your children. If the child lives with you, state "with me" in the address column; otherwise give city/state/country of child's current residence. If deceased, write "deceased" in the address column. If you need more space, continue on separate paper.

Full name of child	Date of birth	Country of birth	Citizenship	A - Number	Address

Form N-400 (Rev. 07/17/91)N Internet   *Continued on next page*

◯   *Continued on back*   ◯

Part 7.   Additional eligibility factors.

Please answer each of the following questions. If your answer is **"Yes"**, explain on a separate paper.

1.   Are you now, or have you ever been a member of, or in any way connected or associated with the Communist Party, or ever knowingly aided or supported the Communist Party directly, or indirectly through another organization, group or person, or ever advocated, taught, believed in, or knowingly supported or furthered the interests of communism?   Yes   No

2.   During the period March 23, 1933 to May 8, 1945, did you serve in, or were you in any way affiliated with, either directly or indirectly, any military unit, paramilitary unit, police unit, self-defense unit, vigilante unit, citizen unit of the Nazi party or SS, government agency or office, extermination camp, concentration camp, prisoner of war camp, prison, labor camp, detention camp or transit camp, under the control or affiliated with:

   a.   The Nazi Government of Germany?   Yes   No

   b.   Any government in any area occupied by, allied with, or established with the assistance or cooperation of, the Nazi Government of Germany?   Yes   No

3.   Have you at any time, anywhere, ever ordered, incited, assisted, or otherwise participated in the persecution of any person because of race, religion, national origin, or political opinion?   Yes   No

4.   Have you ever left the United States to avoid being drafted into the U.S. Armed Forces?   Yes   No

5.   Have you ever failed to comply with Selective Service laws?   Yes   No

   If you have registered under the Selective Service laws, complete the following information:

   Selective Service Number:_____   Date Registered:_____

   If you registered before 1978, also provide the following:

   Local Board Number:_____   Classification:_____

6.   Did you ever apply for exemption from military service because of alienage, conscientious objections or other reasons?   Yes   No

7.   Have you ever deserted from the military, air or naval forces of the United States?   Yes   No

8.   Since becoming a permanent resident, have you ever failed to file a federal income tax return?   Yes   No

9.   Since becoming a permanent resident, have you filed a federal income tax return as a nonresident or failed to file a federal return because you considered yourself to be a nonresident?   Yes   No

10   Are deportation proceedings pending against you, or have you ever been deported, or ordered deported, or have you ever applied for suspension of deportation?   Yes   No

11.   Have you ever claimed in writing, or in any way, to be a United States citizen?   Yes   No

12.   Have you ever:

   a.   been a habitual drunkard?   Yes   No

   b.   advocated or practiced polygamy?   Yes   No

   c.   been a prostitute or procured anyone for prostitution?   Yes   No

   d.   knowingly and for gain helped any alien to enter the U.S. illegally?   Yes   No

   e.   been an illicit trafficker in narcotic drugs or marijuana?   Yes   No

   f.   received income from illegal gambling?   Yes   No

   g.   given false testimony for the purpose of obtaining any immigration benefit?   Yes   No

13.   Have you ever been declared legally incompetent or have you ever been confined as a patient in a mental institution?   Yes   No

14.   Were you born with, or have you acquired in same way, any title or order of nobility in any foreign State?   Yes   No

15.   Have you ever:

   a.   knowingly committed any crime for which you have not been arrested?   Yes   No

   b.   been arrested, cited, charged, indicted, convicted, fined or imprisoned for breaking or violating any law or ordinance excluding traffic regulations?   Yes   No

(If you answer yes to 15, in your explanation give the following information for each incident or occurrence the **city**, **state**, and **country**, where the offense took place, the **date** and **nature** of the offense, and the **outcome** or **disposition** of the case).

Part 8.   Allegiance to the U.S.

If your answer to any of the following questions is **"NO"**, attach a full explanation:

1.   Do you believe in the Constitution and form of government of the U.S.?   Yes   No

2.   Are you willing to take the full Oath of Allegiance to the U.S.? (see instructions)   Yes   No

3.   If the law requires it, are you willing to bear arms on behalf of the U.S.?   Yes   No

4.   If the law requires it, are you willing to perform noncombatant services in the Armed Forces of the U.S.?   Yes   No

5.   If the law requires it, are you willing to perform work of national importance under civilian direction?   Yes   No

Form N-400 (Rev. 07/17/91)N Internet   *Continued on back*

Part 9. Memberships and organizations.

A. List your present and past membership in or affiliation with every organization, association, fund, foundation, party, club, society, or similar group in the United States or in any other place. Include any military service in this part. If none, write "none". Include the name of organization, location, dates of membership and the nature of the organization. If additional space is needed, use separate paper.

Part 10. Complete only if you checked block " C " in Part 2.

How many of your parents are U.S. citizens?   One   Both   (Give the following about one U.S. citizen parent:)

Family Name	Given Name	Middle Name

Address

Basis for citizenship:
   Birth
   Naturalization Cert. No.

Relationship to you (check one):   natural parent   adoptive parent
parent of child legitimated after birth

If adopted or legitimated after birth, give date of adoption or, legitimation: *(month/day/year)* _____.

Does this parent have legal custody of you?   Yes   No

Attach a copy of relating evidence to establish that you are the child of this U.S. citizen and evidence of this parent's citizenship.)

Part 11. Signature. *(Read the information on penalties in the instructions before completing this section).*

I certify or, if outside the United States, I swear or affirm, under penalty of perjury under the laws of the United States of America that this application, and the evidence submitted with it, is all true and correct. I authorize the release of any information from my records which the Immigration and Naturalization Service needs to determine eligibility for the benefit I am seeking.

Signature   Date

Please Note: If you do not completely fill out this form, or fail to submit required documents listed in the instructions, you may not be found eligible for naturalization and this application may be denied.

Part 12. Signature of person preparing form if other than above. *(Sign below)*

I declare that I prepared this application at the request of the above person and it is based on all information of which I have knowledge.

Signature   Print Your Name   Date

Firm Name
and Address

DO NOT COMPLETE THE FOLLOWING UNTIL INSTRUCTED TO DO SO AT THE INTERVIEW

I swear that I know the contents of this application, and supplemental pages 1 through____, that the corrections , numbered 1 through____, were made at my request, and that this amended application, is true to the best of my knowledge and belief.

_____ ____
(Complete and true signature of applicant)

Subscribed and sworn to before me by the applicant.

_____
(Examiner's Signature)   Date

Form N-400 (Rev. 07/17/91)N Internet